An Unauthorized Biography

Johnny
Cash

"The Man in Black"

Read about other

American REBELS

James Dean
*"Dream As If You'll
Live Forever"*

0-7660-2537-3

Kurt Cobain
*"Oh Well, Whatever,
Nevermind"*

0-7660-2426-1

Jimi Hendrix
"Kiss The Sky"

0-7660-2449-0

Madonna
"Express Yourself"

0-7660-2442-3

American REBELS

An Unauthorized Biography

Johnny Cash

" The Man in Black "

Edward Willett

Enslow Publishers, Inc.
40 Industrial Road
Box 398
Berkeley Heights, NJ 07922
USA

http://www.enslow.com

Library of Congress Cataloging-in-Publication Data

Willett, Edward, 1959-
  Johnny Cash : "the man in black" / Edward Willett.
      p. cm. — (American rebels)
  Includes bibliographical references and index.
  Summary: "A biography of country singer Johnny Cash, discussing his early struggles with poverty, rise to fame, personal hardships, and legacy"—Provided by publisher.
  ISBN 978-0-7660-3386-3
  1. Cash, Johnny—Juvenile literature. 2. Country musicians—United States—Biography—Juvenile literature. I. Title.
  ML3930.C27W55 2010
  782.421642092—dc22
  [B]
                                      2009017346

Printed in the United States of America

052010 Lake Book Manufacturing, Inc., Melrose Park, IL

10 9 8 7 6 5 4 3 2 1

Illustration Credits: Associated Press, pp. 6, 14, 23, 66, 88, 98, 104, 113, 127; Everett Collection, pp. 11, 25, 39, 56, 75, 82, 94, 130; Daniel Hartwig, p. 35; Michael Ochs Archives/Getty Images, p. 49; M. Matlock, p. 88 (inset); Redferns, p. 69; John Sommers/Reuters/Landov, p. 123.

Cover Illustration: Associated Press.

Contents

Introduction 6

1 Early Days 10

2 The Music Starts 21

3 The Hits Begin 37

4 Downhill Slide 54

5 Clean and Sober 65

6 The Low Point 84

7 The Final Comeback 101

8 Fade to Black 111

9 The Cash Legacy 125

Chronology 133

Discography 138

Glossary 140

Chapter Notes 142

Further Reading 156

Internet Addresses 157

Index 158

On January 13, 1968, Johnny Cash performed at the Folsom Prison in California.

Introduction

On January 13, 1968, a gray, gloomy Saturday, Johnny Cash entered Folsom State Prison in Repressa, California. With him were a crowd of musicians, technicians, photographers, and reporters. Cash was about to do something no one had ever done before: record a live album in front of a crowd of prisoners.

With more than thirty-five hundred inmates crowded into five enormous cell blocks, Folsom State Prison, the state's second-oldest prison, held some of California's worst offenders. About two thousand prisoners assembled in the dining hall to hear the first of two shows. Armed guards patrolled overhead on walkways. The prisoners couldn't be left in darkness, so the bright neon lights remained on throughout the concert.

Marshall Grant, Cash's longtime bass player, intended to bring Cash onstage with a big dramatic introduction as he always did, but Cash's new producer, Bob Johnston, had other ideas. "All you gotta do," he told Cash, "is walk out there and jerk your head around and say 'Hello. I'm Johnny Cash.'"[1] Cash, he thought, "needed to assert control right from the start."[2]

Cash took his advice. He walked out, grabbed the microphone, and said, "Hello. I'm Johnny Cash."

It would become one of the most famous phrases in the history of American music.

The audience of prisoners exploded. Cash's songs kept them at a high pitch of excitement and appreciation. He sang songs they could identify with, songs about prison and crime, loneliness and separation—and a few just for fun.

Unlike an audience on the outside, the prisoners didn't just respond at the end of the song. Instead, they applauded whenever they heard a line they particularly identified with. Five tape machines running simultaneously in a truck in the prison yard captured their noisy appreciation and helped make not just a great live album, but what is generally considered one of the best live albums ever made.[3]

The album sold 6 million copies. It reached number 13 on the pop charts. It led directly to the equally popular *Johnny Cash at San Quentin*, which in turn led to Johnny Cash hosting his own television show on ABC. In 1969, Columbia Records announced that Johnny Cash had sold more records in the United States that year than the Beatles.

Johnny Cash at Folsom Prison also solidified the public's perception of Johnny Cash as an outlaw, a rebel who followed his own path, no matter what the cost.

Thirty years later, his reputation as a rebel *with* a cause—the cause of the ordinary man—led to an amazing comeback, as he released acclaimed albums that found a whole new audience among listeners who hadn't even been born when he recorded at Folsom Prison.

But the Folsom Prison recording itself was an amazing comeback. At the time he recorded it, many people thought Johnny Cash was already washed up, a has-been who looked old before his time due to years of hard touring and drug abuse.

For Johnny Cash, the road to Folsom Prison and beyond was a rocky one. It began in the darkest years of the Great Depression, in one of the hardest-hit states: Arkansas.

Chapter 1

Early Days

Johnny Cash was born on February 26, 1932, in Kingsland, Arkansas. He was the third son of Ray Cash and Carrie Rivers.

Ray Cash was from the nearby town of Rison. He had met Carrie in 1919 while he was working cutting lumber near Kingsland. During his time there, he boarded with Carrie's parents, John and Rosanna. He was twenty-two and she was fifteen, but despite the age difference they married just a year later, on August 18, 1920. Their first son, Roy, was born in 1921. Their daughter, Margaret Louise, came along three years later, and their second son, Jack, was born in 1929.

When Johnny Cash was born, his mother wanted to name him John, after her father. Ray, on the other hand, wanted to name him Ray. When they couldn't agree, they simply named him J. R.

Ray Cash was a sharecropper, a farmer who didn't own his land, but was allowed to use it in exchange for

Johnny Cash in 1942 at eleven years old.

sharing part of the crop with the landowner. Cash farmed cotton, but after the Great Depression hit, he couldn't make a living at it. Between 1928 and 1932, the price of a five-hundred-pound bale of cotton dropped from $125 to $25.[1]

Johnny Cash recalled later that Ray Cash had to take on whatever work he could find, wherever he could find it. He worked at a sawmill. He cleared land. He laid railroad track. "He did every kind of work imaginable, from painting to shoveling to herding cattle."[2]

When Ray Cash couldn't find work, he'd hunt, feeding his family with small game like rabbits,

The Great Depression

When the stock market crashed on October 29, 1929, it triggered the Great Depression. It was the worst economic collapse in modern history. Banks failed, businesses closed, and more than 15 million Americans, one-quarter of the workforce, lost their jobs.

President Herbert Hoover called it "a passing incident." He was wrong: it would last until the 1940s.

In 1932, Franklin Delano Roosevelt was elected president on the promise of a "New Deal" for Americans to help deal with the ravages of the Depression. The Dyess Colony where Johnny Cash grew up was just one of many government programs aimed at helping people cope.

In an era when women typically didn't have jobs outside the home, men were expected to provide for their wives and children. That made not being able to find work particularly hard on husbands and fathers, who found it humiliating to have to ask for assistance.[3]

squirrels, and opossum. And sometimes, when he had to, he'd ride the rails, traveling "in boxcars, going from one harvest to another to try to make a little money picking fruits or vegetables."[4]

"Our house was right on the railroad tracks, out in the woods, and one of my earliest memories is of seeing him jump out of a moving boxcar and roll down the ditch in front of our door," Cash wrote in his second autobiography, published in 1997.[5]

A New Deal

Then in 1934 the family got a chance at a better life. President Franklin D. Roosevelt had set up the Federal Emergency Relief Administration to help Americans hard hit by the Depression. Among its programs was one that offered to relocate needy families to a brand-new model community. Originally known as Colonization Project Number One, the new community was later renamed Dyess, after an Arkansas government administrator.

Dyess was built on sixteen thousand acres of reclaimed swampland in Mississippi County, Arkansas. It had a town hall, a movie theater, a cotton mill, a cannery, churches, shops, a school, and a hospital. Families relocated to Dyess would each receive a brand-new house, twenty acres of land to clear and farm, a barn, a mule, a milk cow, and a hen coop.[6]

To apply, families had to answer questions covering everything from their debts to their church preference, farming experience, and club affiliations. Initially the Cashes were told they hadn't been accepted, but for

Johnny Cash grew up in this home in Dyess, Arkansas.

some reason that decision was reversed, and on March 23, 1935, a truck arrived to carry the family from Kingsland to Dyess. J. R., his father, his two brothers, and the family's belongings rode in the back under a tarpaulin. J. R.'s mother and his two sisters (his second sister, Reba, had been born the year before) rode up front next to the driver.

The 250-mile drive took a day and a half on narrow and muddy roads. Cash said the first song he could remember singing was "I Am Bound for the Promised Land," as he bounced in the back of the truck.[7] On March 24, the family arrived at House 266 on the dirt track known as Road Three. There they found "a newly built five-room house, a barn, a mule, a chicken coop, (a) smokehouse and an outdoor toilet. No plumbing, no electricity."[8] But it was theirs. For the Cashes, it really did look like the promised land.

Settling in Dyess

The Dyess Colony families were expected to be largely self-sufficient, growing their own food. However, they were also expected to grow cotton, which they sold collectively, sharing in any profits from the cotton gin and the store.

As Ray Cash and his oldest son, Roy, cleared the land of the thick vegetation that covered it, the three younger children played and Carrie Cash gardened. She grew the fruits and vegetables the family would need for the next winter, then canned them at the community cannery. Home economists from the government taught canning, cooking, dressmaking, and other homemaking skills to the new colonists. Children received regular medical checkups. Dyess, Johnny said later, was really a "socialistic setup."[9]

Ray Cash had to make a yearly payment of $111.41 on his house and land. He made each one promptly. Each farmer also received an advance payment on his crops each year. Cash was one of the few who always repaid that advance on time. Thanks to his hard work, by 1940, he had enough money to make a down payment on a farm next door, which doubled his land from twenty to forty-five acres. By 1945, he owned both his land and house.[10]

At times the land itself seemed to be working against him. In January 1937, the nearby Tyronza River and one of the main drainage ditches flooded. Carrie and the younger children were evacuated to Kingsland. Ray and Roy tried to stay at the house, but after a week they had to leave, too.

When the Cashes returned home on February 16, they found their house covered with silt. Snakes were living in the barn and hens had laid eggs on the living room sofa. Driftwood littered the land. But the farm survived. In fact, Ray thought the silt actually improved the soil. Afterward, he was able to harvest two bales of cotton per acre, along with soybeans and corn.

Starting School and Starting Work

The year after the flood, 1938, J. R. Cash turned six years old and got a new baby sister, Joanne. He also started school. When he wasn't in school, though, he was expected to help out in the cotton field. He started out carrying water to the bigger workers, but as he grew older, he picked cotton alongside his father and older siblings.

Picking cotton and stuffing it into a six-foot-long canvas sack he had to drag along behind him was hard work. Ray Cash made it even harder. He wouldn't let anyone slack off, and he had a quick, hot temper. According to Cash biographer Michael Streissguth, when Roy Cash, J. R.'s oldest brother, made a mistake or was impertinent, his father would rip the leather reins off the mule and whip him.[11]

Johnny Cash always said his father never laid a hand on him, but he admitted his father verbally abused him more than once. His father could be harsh in other ways. When J. R. was four years old, he made a pet out of a stray dog. About a year later, Ray shot the dog in the head with a .22. He didn't tell his sons about it until they found the body. He claimed the dog had been eating scraps intended for fattening the hogs.

"I thought my world had ended that morning, that nothing was safe, that life wasn't safe," Cash wrote in his second autobiography. "It was a frightening thing, and it took a long time for me to get over it."[12]

Aside from the movie theater, Dyess didn't offer much culture. But at least it had music. People sang as they worked in the fields. In the Road Fifteen Church of God that Carrie made J. R. attend, guitars, mandolins, and banjos would sometimes accompany the music.

Music Takes Hold

All that music began to take hold of J. R.'s soul. After his father bought a battery-operated radio, the house was full of music. On Sundays it was mostly church music, but the rest of the week it was country music. The first song Cash remembered hearing on the radio was "Hobo Bill's Last Ride," the sorry tale of a hobo who died of neglect. Sometimes the signals drifted in from such faraway places as Cincinnati and Chicago.

17

Ray Cash thought J. R. was wasting time when he listened to the radio. Carrie Cash, however, loved music. She played the piano in church and sang to the children in the evenings. Her father had taught singing, and she wanted her family to have music in their lives as they grew up just as she had.[13] The family had expanded again with the birth of a final child, Tommy, in 1940.

"We sang in the house, on the porch, everywhere," Cash remembered. "We sang in the fields . . . I'd start it off with pop songs I'd heard on the radio, and my sister Louise and I would challenge each other: 'Bet you don't know this one!' Usually I knew them and I'd join in well before she'd finished."[14]

Roy Cash, J. R.'s big brother, even played in a band. The Delta Rhythm Ramblers, an amateur band made up of him and four schoolmates, won first place in a local talent contest in 1939, the year J. R. was seven. But the Second World War ended Roy's brief musical career. The Delta Rhythm Ramblers broke up in 1941 as its members were drafted into the armed forces. Roy himself joined the Navy.

After Roy left, J. R.'s next-oldest brother, Jack, became his mentor.

J. R. and Jack

Jack impressed everyone who met him. Even though he was just a young teenager, he was already talking about becoming a Baptist minister. J. R., two years younger, idolized him. Not only did Jack seem tougher and smarter than everyone else, but he also seemed more

Christian. "There was nobody in the world as good and as wise and as strong as my big brother Jack," Cash wrote years later.[15]

J. R. went to church twice on Sundays and attended Bible study every Wednesday night. Influenced by that and by Jack's example, early in 1944 he decided give his life to Christ. He was twelve years old, the "age of accountability," when a child is old enough to decide whether or not he will be a Christian.

As the congregation at First Baptist Church in Dyess sang the old hymn "Just As I Am" on February 26, 1944, J. R. walked down the aisle to

"I felt brand-new, born again."

the front of the church. Jack was sitting in the front row. J. R. took the preacher's hand, then knelt at the altar. "It was like a birthday rolling around," he wrote in his first autobiography. "I felt brand-new, born again."[16] He also felt closer to Jack than ever before.

But then came Saturday, May 12, 1944.

J. R. decided to go fishing in one of the large drainage ditches. He asked Jack to go with him, but Jack refused. Jack was heading to the school workshop, where he earned extra money by cutting fence posts.

The two brothers started out walking together, then separated. About noon J. R. headed for home. As he reached the place where he and Jack had split up, he saw a Model A Ford heading toward him. The preacher was driving. J. R.'s father was with him. Ray Cash told J. R. to throw away his fishing pole and get in, and J. R. knew something terrible had happened.

As they drove on, Ray told J. R. that Jack had been badly hurt. He'd been pulled onto the circular saw in the school workshop. The blade had ripped through his clothes and into his stomach.

Jack lingered for a few days. On May 20, he asked his mother whether she could hear the angels singing. He told her he could hear them, and that was where he was going. Then he died. "After Jack's death I felt like I'd died, too," Cash wrote in his second autobiography. "I was terribly lonely without him. I had no other friend."[17]

Even worse, J. R.'s father blamed him for Jack's death. "Ray told him bluntly that he should have died rather than his faithful brother, and he had no business going fishing while Jack was out working for the family," Steve Turner wrote in his authorized biography, *The Man Called Cash*.[18]

The tragedy, his own guilt, and his father's accusation had one positive outcome: it kick-started J. R.'s creativity. "It's when I really started writing," Cash said. "I was trying to put down what I was feeling."[19]

"Putting down what he was feeling" would eventually make Johnny Cash one of the greatest American songwriters in history.

But in 1944, his first steps along the road to fame were still more than a decade away.

Chapter 2

The Music Starts

J. R.'s mother had ordered a guitar from Sears &
Roebuck sometime before Jack's death, but it disappeared
at about the same time as he died. Probably, Cash realized
later, it was sold to help the family get through hard
financial times. Not only had they lost the extra income
Jack had been bringing in, but they also had doctor's bills
to pay.

Without a guitar of his own, J. R. turned to Jesse
"Pete" Barnhill, a boy a year ahead of him at school, to
learn to play. Barnhill's right hand had been withered by
childhood polio, so to play his Gibson flat-top guitar he
chorded with his left hand and just beat the rhythm
with his right.[1] "Pete was crazy for music the way I
was," Cash wrote, "and we were both crazy for the
radio."[2] Barnhill played songs by country artists like
Hank Snow, Ernest Tubb, and Jimmie Rodgers, and
they'd sing them together.

J. R.'s mother believed his voice was a gift from God. She wanted him to have singing lessons. "She was determined that I was going to leave the farm and do well in life," he said. "And she thought, with the gift I might be able to do that."[3] Each singing lesson cost three dollars, and to pay for them, J. R.'s mother started doing other people's laundry. It took her a full day of work to earn the money for one lesson.

Despite his mother's sacrifice, J. R. didn't have much use for the idea of singing lessons until he went to his first one and discovered that the teacher, LaVanda Mae Fielder of nearby Lepanto, Arkansas, was very nice, very young, and, best of all, very pretty. But halfway through the third lesson, after listening to J. R. sing popular ballads like "Drink to Me Only With Thine Eyes" and "I'll Take You Home Again, Kathleen," Fielder closed the piano and asked him to sing a song he really wanted to sing, without accompaniment. J. R. sang Hank Williams's "Long Gone Lonesome Blues."

> **LaVanda Mae Fielder told him to never take voice lessons again.**

When he was done, Fielder told him to never take voice lessons again. "Don't let me or anyone else change the way you sing," she said.[4]

"I was pretty happy about that," Cash said. "I didn't really want to change, you know. I felt good about my voice."[5] He took her advice: he never took voice lessons again.

But he kept singing. He'd take long walks down the dark night roads around Dyess, humming the songs he heard on the radio. "It was pitch dark on the gravel road, or if the moon was shining, the shadows were even scarier," he wrote. "But I sang all the way home . . . I sang through the dark, and I decided that that kind of music was going to be my magic to take me through all the dark places."[6]

High School Days

Although Cash later wrote that Jack had been his only friend, in fact he was fairly popular in high school. At least, the girls liked him. Louise Nichols, whom he claimed was his first girlfriend, remembered him as "something special."

"Everybody loved him," she said. "Everybody!"[7]

Sue Moore, who dated J. R. when he was in his senior year and she was fifteen, said, "I thought he was a hunk . . . A nice, lovable guy."[8]

Nadine Johnson, whom he also dated that year, said, "I think what attracted me to him was that he was so well-liked."[9]

But although he was generally a typical high school boy, playing practical jokes and occasionally getting into fights, sometimes, his friends noted, J. R. was "kind of off on another planet."[10] Sometimes when they were harvesting cotton, his sister Louise

Johnny Cash in his senior class photo

23

would ask him something and get no answer. "I'd look over at him and his mind seemed to be far away."[11]

"It seemed like he was going somewhere," remembered his friend A. J. Henson. "He was on a journey."[12]

"Far away" was exactly where Johnny Cash knew he wanted to be as his high school years wound down. So did most of his classmates. The post-war boom in the economy was creating new opportunities for manufacturing work in cities all over North America. As well, a generation of veterans had come back from the Second World War with stories of the rest of the world. For restless young people, living in Dyess and growing cotton for the rest of their lives held little appeal. "When we grew up, it was second nature that we wouldn't live in Dyess when we were grown," Cash said. "It was the aim of every person to get a better job."[13]

During his last year in school, J. R. was elected class vice president and an officer in the school's chapter of the Future Farmers of America, though he had no intention of taking up farming. But he also kept singing. At his graduation ceremony on May 19, 1950, he performed "Drink to Me Only With Thine Eyes," one of the songs he'd learned in one of his three voice lessons.

But even though he could sing a little, he was hardly in a position to launch a musical career. He could only play a couple of chords on the guitar. He'd only ever been to two concerts: he'd heard the Louvin Brothers

The Carter Family in the 1950s. From left to right: Maybelle Carter (sitting), June Carter (standing far left), Anita Carter, and Helen Carter.

perform in the Dyess High School auditorium, and he'd gone to the Grand Ole Opry in Nashville on a school trip. There he saw the Carter Family perform—and was particularly taken with the youngest Carter daughter, a girl by the name of June.[14]

Looking for Work

With graduation behind him, Cash looked for work. He hitchhiked to Bald Knob, Arkansas, and picked strawberries for three days. Then, like thousands of other southerners, he headed north in search of work in the automobile factories of Michigan. With him were a barber from Dyess, Frank Kinney, and a school friend, Milton Stansbury. They arrived in Pontiac, Michigan, about midnight after a twenty-four-hour bus ride. At 8:00 A.M. they went down to the Fisher Body plant. At 4:00 P.M. they went to work.

Cash stamped metal into car hoods on the assembly line. He earned a dollar and a half an hour, but he hated the monotonous work. He felt completely out of his element. After he cut his right forearm on a hood, he quit. He'd only been working for three weeks, so he was back in Dyess just a little more than a month after his graduation.

Ray Cash, struggling to make ends meet, was working at the Proctor and Gamble margarine factory in nearby Evadale. Cash joined his father there for two weeks. But then, on June 25, 1950, North Korea invaded South Korea. Within a few days, American troops were involved in combat.

Cash Joins the Air Force . . . and Meets Vivian

Along with every other boy who had turned eighteen, Cash had already been registered for the draft. Via a lottery, the draft selected young men between the ages of eighteen and twenty-six to serve in the armed forces. If you were drafted, you had no choice as to which branch of the service—army, navy, air force, or marines—you would serve in. If you volunteered, however, you could choose the branch you preferred.

26

Like many other young men hoping to avoid the infantry, Cash decided his best option was to volunteer. On July 5, Cash traveled to Blythesville, Arkansas, and enlisted in the United States Air Force for a four-year stint.

Afterward, he not only had a new job, but he also had a new name. When he'd registered for the draft he'd had to give a first and middle name, even though he didn't really have either: just the initials J. R. He wrote in John Ray, and so once he joined the air force, John Ray Cash he became.

Cash was formally inducted on July 7, 1950, in Little Rock, Arkansas. Later that summer Cash's family drove him to Memphis, where he boarded a train for San Antonio, Texas, to begin his training at Lackland Air Base.

Cash's instructors discovered he had an aptitude for radio work: not for repairing them, but for sitting for hours at a receiver recording transmissions he heard. As a result, after two months of basic training, Cash was sent to Keesler Air Force Base in Biloxi, Mississippi, to study Morse code, typing, and electronics. He was one of the best students in the course, which led to him being recruited by the newly formed Twelfth Radio Squadron Mobile (RSM).

Cash graduated from Keesler on April 27, 1951. For the next eight weeks, he took advanced training at Brooks Air Force Base in Texas. At the roller-skating rink in Brooks one day, he met a pretty, bronze-skinned seventeen-year-old Italian girl named Vivian Liberto. They dated for the rest of his stay in Brooks.

When his training in Brooks finished, Cash went to Dyess for a month's leave. After that he headed north again to meet up with the rest of the Twelfth RSM before boarding a ship for West Germany, where he would be monitoring radio transmissions from the Soviet Union.

He wouldn't see Vivian Liberto for almost three years, but she was destined to become his first wife.

Life in West Germany

After their ship docked at Bremerhaven, in northern Germany, the men of the Twelfth RSM traveled by train

Post-war Germany

When Cash arrived in West Germany, the Second World War had only been over for six years. As they traveled across the country, the Americans saw collapsed bridges, the blackened ruins of factories and houses, and bombed-out churches.

Although it had never been bombed, Landsberg had played a central role in the war. At least eleven concentration camps were located in the surrounding area. Adolf Hitler had written *Mein Kampf*, the book that gave rise to the Nazi Party, while imprisoned in Landsberg in the 1920s. War criminals were still being held and executed in that same prison. Cash's own air base was a former Luftwaffe (German air force) base.

It must have been an eye-opening experience for a young man who until a few months before had seldom been out of tiny, rural Dyess.

to Landsberg, a town of about ten thousand people near Munich, in the southern part of the country.

The work the Twelfth RSM did in Landsberg was highly classified, so its members didn't really mingle with the other men on the base. Cash and his colleagues worked eight-hour shifts in a windowless room on the top floor of a three-story building. There they sat at radio receivers, earphones clamped to their heads, straining to hear, above the static, the dots and dashes of Morse code coming from over the airwaves from the Soviet Union and its satellite nations, including East Germany, occupied by the Soviets since the end of the war. Since everything was in code, they had no idea what they were hearing. They simply wrote it all down and passed the results along to analysts who would try to decipher it. Cash proved to be one of the unit's most capable operators, and as a result was eventually promoted to staff sergeant.

During his time in Germany, Cash at first tried to live true to his strict upbringing. He didn't drink and hung out with other men who didn't drink. He spent a lot of time playing and singing old songs, especially gospel songs, with other homesick soldiers, most of whom were more accomplished musicians than he was. Playing with them, Cash improved his own guitar playing.

Cash also started writing his own songs for the first time, including his first gospel song, "Belshazzar." The military newspaper *Stars and Stripes* published the

Cash also started writing his own songs for the first time, including his first gospel song, "Belshazzar."

words to his song "Hey, Porter." Cash also wrote short stories and liked to draw.

Cash didn't stay a nondrinker. Practically everybody in Germany drank beer, so he started drinking that. From beer, he wrote, "I graduated to German Cognac and having more wild times . . . I took a part in most everything else that goes along with drunkenness that last year in Germany."[15]

Nevertheless, those that were in the service with him remember him regularly attending the Protestant chapel, praying each day and reading the Bible.[16]

After every six days of duty, the men were given a three-day pass. Cash used those passes to see a lot of Europe. He visited Paris, Venice, Zurich, London, Salzburg, Amsterdam, and Berlin, among other places. Throughout his time in Germany, Cash wrote a steady stream of letters to Vivian Liberto, sometimes two or three a day.

Back in the U.S.A.

Cash returned to the United States early in the summer of 1954. On July 3, he was honorably discharged. A little over a month later, on August 7, he married Vivian in San Antonio.

Between his return and his marriage, Cash looked for a job and an apartment in Memphis, where his brother Roy, sister Reba, and other people he knew from Dyess had moved. After considering (and rejecting) police

The Strange Inspiration for a Hit

Although he didn't write the song in West Germany, one of Cash's iconic hits, "I Walk the Line," had its beginning there.

Cash said that one day he returned to his quarters to discover someone had been playing around with his tape recorder. When he rewound the tape and pressed play, he heard strange sounds, including a voice that seemed to say "Father."

Cash asked around to find out who had done it, and discovered someone had put a tape on the recorder upside down and backwards. The other man had been strumming chords on his guitar, and halfway through he said "turn it off," which sounded like "father" backward.

"It sounded like a religious ceremony or something," he said. The resulting chord progression "broke all the musical laws in history," Cash said, but it stayed in his head, and would later become the tune for "I Walk the Line."[17]

work, he ended up selling appliances door-to-door for the Home Equipment Company. He had no intention of being a door-to-door salesman all his life, though. Sometime while in Germany, where he began writing his own songs and playing music with a group called the Landsberg Barbarians, he'd begun to dream of life as a musician.

One time-honored method of breaking into the music business was to start as a radio announcer. With that in mind, Cash applied for an announcer's job in Corinth, Tennessee, eighty miles east of Memphis. The station director, John Bell, told him that with his twangy

Arkansas accent he'd never make it as an announcer without more training. He suggested Cash check out Keegan's School of Broadcasting in Memphis. Cash followed his advice and signed up for a part-time course, two mornings a week for ten months.[18]

In September 1954, Cash and Vivian moved into a two-bedroom, second-floor apartment. It had a private bathroom, but a shared kitchen. Within a few months, Cash had made enough money as a salesman that he and Vivian moved to a larger apartment not far from where he worked. By that time, Vivian was pregnant with their first child.

Making Music in Memphis

Memphis was full of music, and it kept calling to Cash. "I spent more time in my car listening to the radio than I did knocking on doors," he wrote later.[19]

But he wasn't just listening to music. He was also making it. Almost as soon as he arrived from Germany, Roy introduced him to two automobile mechanics he worked with, Marshall Grant and Luther Perkins, both of whom also played guitar and sang.

"We three became friends and 'made music' together practically every night at Roy's house or at mine," he said. "We'd sing and play until the early hours of the morning, night after night."[20] They began to think about trying to make a record.

The three soon decided that they couldn't hope to impress a record producer if they were all playing rhythm guitar, so Perkins switched to lead electric guitar and Grant to bass. Since Cash did most of the singing, he would stick to rhythm guitar. After about four months, the unnamed trio played its first public performance in a Memphis church. After that, they played a fund-raiser at a Bob's Barbecue restaurant for Ralph Johnson, a powerboat racer and friend of Grant's who'd been injured in a collision.

> **Memphis was full of music, and it kept calling to Cash.**

Their first paying gig was for the Hurst Motor Company: they received fifty dollars for cruising Union Avenue, playing on the back of a flatbed truck. For three months they also played a (nonpaying) regular Saturday afternoon slot on KWEM Radio, sponsored by Cash's employer, Home Equipment, until their growing number of live engagements ate up their time.

The First Johnny Cash Record

Playing live was one thing, but what they really needed to make a music career was a record.

Sam Phillips had launched Sun Records in 1952. Its name reflected his sense of optimism, of a new day and a new beginning. He'd rented a small space at 706 Union Avenue for his studio. Memphis swarmed with musicians of all kinds, playing everything from boogie-woogie and western swing to gospel, blues, and hillbilly. Phillips was willing to listen to and record anyone he thought was good, no matter what genre they worked in.

In 1954, Phillips discovered Elvis Presley. Presley's success attracted many other artists to Sun, not just

Johnny Cash, but also Carl Perkins and Jerry Lee Lewis. One of Phillips's innovations was the use of drums, which were almost unheard of in country music at the time. Sparse instrumentation with a strong, drum-driven rhythm became the hallmark of a new style of music called "rockabilly," one of the forerunners of modern rock music.

Later artists who got their start at Sun Records included Roy Orbison, Charlie Rich, Bill Justis, and Harold Jenkins (better known as Conway Twitty).[21]

"I was fully confident that I was going to see Sam Phillips and to record for him," Cash recalled. "When I called him, I thought, 'I'm going to get on Sun Records.' So, I called him . . . and he turned me down flat."

He tried again two weeks later, and was turned down again. Cash wanted to record his gospel songs, but Phillips told him he couldn't sell gospel. But finally, Cash said, he went down to the recording studio with his guitar, sat on the front step, and waited for Phillips to arrive. When he did, Cash said, he told him, "I'm John Cash. I'm the one that's been calling. And if you'd listen to me, I believe you'll be glad you did."[22]

Phillips agreed to listen to Cash, Perkins, and Grant play—and was impressed. He let them record "Hey, Porter," one of the songs Cash had written in Germany. For the flip side, he asked Cash to write "a love song, or maybe a bitter weeper."[23] In response, Cash wrote "Cry, Cry, Cry," which Phillips then decided to make the "A" side of the single, the song that would be released first.

Cash made his record "Hey, Porter" in 1955.

They made the record on a Thursday afternoon in May 1955. Phillips had suggested Cash call himself "Johnny" instead of "John," so they dubbed themselves "Johnny Cash and the Tennessee Two."

That same month, on May 24, the Cashes' first daughter, Rosanne, was born.

According to Grant, at first their only ambition was to hear themselves on the radio. When he finally did hear their record played, one morning while driving to work, "I thought that was *it*," he said.[24] But the next day, five stations in Memphis were playing their song. The day after that, all of them were. By the end of the week, all of the stations were playing both sides. After a month, stations across the South were playing it, and the record climbed to number 14 on the country music charts.

With the success of that first record, offers for live gigs started rolling in. Cash wrote to his friend Ted Freeman in late July that his potential manager thought he could get them five or six nights a week right through the winter, never making "less than $20 a night and lots of night's I'll make $30 or more when we play the bigger towns."

He signed himself "Johnny Cash—the most promising young artist Memphis, Tennessee, has ever produced."

He also wrote, "I believe I can make a pretty good living at it."[25]

As events would quickly prove, he was right.

Chapter 3

The Hits Begin

The "potential manager" Cash had written his friend about was Bob Neal. Neal, a disc jockey for WMPS in Memphis, also owned his own record shop. Since the early 1950s he'd been promoting and emceeing country music shows in the Memphis area. In December of 1954, he'd taken over management of a promising young artist named Elvis Presley.

He wouldn't be Elvis's manager for long. By the summer of 1955 "Colonel" Tom Parker was well on his way to taking over that role. Parker would go on to help make Elvis a superstar.

Neal moved on. He created a booking agency, Stars Incorporated, to exclusively book Sun Records artists. Among the first to sign with Neal were Johnny Cash and the Tennessee Two. By June 1956 Neal had become Cash's personal manager.

Cash vs. Elvis

In the same letter in which he called Neal his potential manager, Cash mentioned he'd be touring with "another boy on Sun"—namely Elvis Presley.[1]

At the time, Presley wasn't any more a superstar than Cash was. The two had a kind of friendly rivalry, each keeping tabs on the other's record sales and concert successes. They even mimicked each other in their performances.

Both of their careers reached a turning point at a concert at Overton Park Shell in Memphis on August 5, 1955, that featured twenty-two acts and drew more than four thousand fans. Elvis had only performed twice in Memphis that year, and the last time he'd played the Overton Park Shell he'd been billed under Slim Whitman. And for Johnny Cash and the Tennessee Two, it was a debut. They were billed under—*way* under—Presley, but Cash later saw it as the show that officially launched his career.[2] Cash performed "Cry, Cry, Cry" and "Hey, Porter," and then for an encore a song he'd recorded but hadn't yet released, "Folsom Prison Blues." Then he stood backstage and watched Elvis perform as "the girls and women screamed, cried, and fainted."

"Though the men might be jealous, nobody could keep from watching him," Cash remembered. "He had . . . a personal magnetism on and offstage—but especially onstage—that is unique."[3]

Johnny Cash (left) and Elvis Presley, circa 1955

The next day, the only two photos of the show in the Memphis Press-Scimitar were of Elvis Presley and Johnny Cash.

Presley wasn't the only star or soon-to-be star from the Sun Records stable that Cash met in those early days. Carl Perkins, famous for "Blue Suede Shoes" (which Elvis later recorded, too), became one of Cash's "longest, truest" friends.[4] He met Jerry Lee Lewis around the same time, and Roy Orbison soon after.

Cash's friendship with Perkins paid off in a big way when they were both booked on a show in Gladewater, Texas (with Presley as the headliner). Cash was playing with the peculiar riff he'd heard on the twisted tape in Germany, and mentioned to Perkins that he wanted to write a song about being true to himself, his wife, and God. He sang him the first verse, and said it was called "Because You're Mine."[5]

"Y'know, 'I Walk the Line' would be a better title," Perkins said.[6]

"The lyrics came as fast as I could write, and in twenty minutes I had it finished," Cash remembered.[7]

Cash and the Tennessee Two were popular, but audiences didn't react nearly as strongly to them as they did to Presley. Partly, they didn't know what to make of the trio's unique sound. "There's been times when we'd do maybe a song or two . . . and people would stand there and look at you with the mouth open because they hadn't

> **"Y'know, 'I Walk the Line' would be a better title," Perkins said.**

never heard anything like us, because there hadn't been anything like us," Marshall Grant said.[8]

Louisiana Hayride and "Folsom Prison Blues"

One place they did get a great reception was on the radio program *Louisiana Hayride*, broadcast out of Shreveport's Municipal Auditorium by radio station KWKH. The program could be picked up as far west as California. Sometimes CBS and Armed Forces Radio would carry part of the show, too. It had helped launch Elvis Presley's career, and it helped launch Cash's, too. Both of his performances drew encores at his debut performance on December 3. Cash called the reaction "intoxicating," and he signed to appear every Saturday night for a year.[9]

A Fateful Decision?

The morning after their tumultuous reception on *Louisiana Hayride* was a Sunday. Cash was riding in a car with Grant and Perkins, and suddenly felt a pang when he realized he should be in church.

Grant offered to stop at one along the way, but Cash decided they should keep on driving. They had a show to do that night and had to get on down the road.

Later Cash pinpointed his decision that morning as a fateful one that left him "vulnerable and easy prey for all the temptations and destructive vices that the backstage of the entertainment world has to offer."[10]

41

On December 15, 1955, Sun Records released Cash's brand-new single, "Folsom Prison Blues." It drove his popularity to new heights.

"There was nothing like it in popular music in 1956," Cash biographer Michael Streissguth wrote. "Compared to Presley's exuberance, Perry Como's urbane whispers, and the Drifters crooning harmonies, Cash and the Tennessee Two's 'Folsom Prison Blues' was rope burn . . . so jagged and raw . . . an unflinching look at an ugly place."[11]

In January 1956, Cash received his first royalty check from Sun for six thousand dollars. Up until then

Folsom Prison Plagiarism?

Johnny Cash wrote "Folsom Prison Blues" while he was still in the air force, when any idea he had of being a musician was still just a vague dream. He lifted the melody, and a lot of the words, from composer Gordon Jenkins's song "Crescent City Blues," on the album *Seven Dreams*.[12]

Although Jenkins let the initial release of the song go unchallenged, he filed a lawsuit after the song was recorded live for the *Johnny Cash at Folsom Prison* album. In the end, he settled out of court for almost a hundred thousand dollars.

Years later, in 1996, Cash said that at the time he wrote the song, "I really had no idea I would be a professional recording artist. I wasn't trying to rip anybody off."[13]

By all accounts, he improved it. "It was pure white-man's blues before Cash got hold of it and injected some soul," is how Cash biographer Michael Streissguth puts it.[14]

42

he'd kept his sales job with Home Equipment Company, despite his busy touring schedule. Now, having just earned more in a single check than his father had ever earned in a year or his brother earned annually as field service representative for Chrysler, he finally felt confident enough to quit.

He hadn't yet turned twenty-four.

The Memphis music scene shot to national attention in 1956. Elvis Presley's contract had been purchased by RCA late in 1955, and his first RCA single, "Heartbreak Hotel," was number one on the charts by April. Carl Perkins's "Blue Suede Shoes" was number 4 in March. And not just on the country charts, either: both artists had broken through into the wider world of pop music. "Blue Suede Shoes" was the first song in history to simultaneously hit the pop, country, and R&B charts.

And then there was Cash. "Folsom Prison Blues" was a top-10 country hit. On April 2, 1956, Cash and the Tennessee Two recorded four more tracks, including "I Walk the Line." Cash originally recorded it as a slow ballad, but Sam Phillips convinced him to pick up the tempo on a late take—and that was the version he sent to radio stations.

> **"Folsom Prison Blues" was a top-10 country hit.**

"When I heard it, I called Sam and asked him not to send out any more because it sounded so awful," Cash said. "But that's the one everybody liked, so all of a sudden I started liking it, too."[15]

43

Phillips used some of the thirty-five thousand dollars he'd gotten from RCA for Presley's contract to promote "I Walk the Line." It climbed to number one on Billboard's country charts. It was Cash's biggest hit for Sun Records, selling more than 2 million copies, and eventually lent its name to the movie version of his life half a century later . . . something he couldn't even have imagined in 1955.

Cash bought a bigger house in a better neighborhood and upgraded his car. His newfound popularity even affected his family. His little brother Tommy, still in high school in Dyess, remembered that suddenly they had become "Johnny Cash's family." Instead of people asking him about his basketball, or his dad about the cotton harvest, they'd wanted to know how Johnny was, and when his new record would be out. "It was a total switch."[16]

The Grand Ole Opry

On July 7, 1956, with "I Walk the Line" climbing the charts, Cash achieved another long-held ambition: he appeared for the first time on the Grand Ole Opry, the most prestigious showcase in country music, constantly scouted by the top recording studios and concert producers.

Although he'd later be known as the "Man in Black," he didn't wear black that night. He wore a white jacket with blue trim that his mother had made, a black shirt, black trousers with a white stripe down the outside seams, and white shoes.[17]

Reporter Ben A. Green, writing for the *Nashville Banner*, said Cash's performance of "I Walk the Line" unleashed a "veritable tornado" of applause. "The boy had struck home, where the heart is," he wrote, and the country audience "had taken a new member into the family."[18]

The story emphasizes that Cash considered himself a "100 per cent" country music artist, and never intended to be anything else. An unnamed "veteran Opry Official" said, "He's one of us."[19]

But in fact, Cash resented the Opry. He didn't like the way it tried to tie him down to pure country. As well, some of the Opry old-timers thought he was too "rock and roll," and they felt rock and roll was for black people, not white people. They made sure he knew how they felt, Cash told *Rolling Stone* in 1992, and when he left that night, he told himself, "I don't wanna go back to this place anymore. I don't have to put up with that crap."[20]

He would go back, but already Cash wanted more of a career than the Opry could give him.

Still, the Opry had already shaped his life in one very important way: it had shown him June Carter for the first time, during that high school trip he'd taken to Nashville. June and her mother and two daughters, performing as the Carter Family, sometimes called "The First Family of Country Music," were at the Grand Ole Opry the night of his debut. Cash found June backstage, went up to her and told her jokingly that one day he'd marry her. She replied, "Good. I can't wait."[21]

"I can't remember anything else we talked about, except his eyes," she wrote decades later, "those black eyes that shone like agates."[22]

Of course, Cash wasn't really going to marry June Carter. His wife, Vivian, had just given birth to their second daughter, Kathy.

On the Road

Thanks to the success of "I Walk the Line" and the exposure provided by the Grand Ole Opry, Cash and the Tennessee Two spent the rest of 1956 on the road. They played in Colorado, Arizona, Pennsylvania, Ohio, and Minnesota. In December they toured California. In April 1957, they headed off on their first tour outside the United States, spending twenty-four days in Canada.

During the California tour, Ralph J. Gleason wrote in the December 16, 1956, edition of the *San Francisco Chronicle* that "if the reaction of the crowd at the performances is any indication, Presley has a rival."[23]

A promoter named Stew Carnall booked the California tour for Cash. He figured so many midwesterners had moved to California during the Depression and war years that there had to be a market there for country music. When Cash proved him right, he bought half of Cash's management contract for five thousand dollars, plus 7 percent of Cash's next annual gross. In effect, he became Cash's tour manager.

That touring just kept intensifying. Besides the concerts, Cash was booked on TV shows, including a ten-show commitment to the popular *Jackie Gleason Show*. It was an important career step. Journalist Robert Johnson called it the "magic door" swinging open and giving Cash "a chance at the glory road," because it was Gleason Enterprises that had helped raise Elvis to national prominence.[24]

Making the grueling schedule worse was the fact that Johnny Cash and the Tennessee Two had to drive themselves wherever they were going, on two-lane roads. And wherever they went, they had to get back to Shreveport almost every Saturday night for the *Louisiana Hayride*.

Cash wrote to his friend Ted Freeman in May 1957, after the tour of Canada, that they had averaged 420 miles per day, that he was twenty-six pounds lighter and ten years older, and that *"I am tired and sick."*[25]

And then, in July 1957, during a tour with Patsy Cline, Ray Price, Ferlin Husky, Faron Young, and Hank Thompson, Young's fiddle player, Gordon Terry, gave Cash a small white tablet.[26]

A Fateful Pill

The tablet was a "Benny," short for Benzedrine. An amphetamine, Benzedrine was a completely legal drug at the time, prescribed by doctors for everything from fatigue to obesity. It provided a burst of energy and a feeling of euphoria and confidence, although restlessness and fatigue followed. In response, you could sleep away most of the next day—or you could take another pill to keep going.

Cash took that first pill en route to Jacksonville, Florida. It woke him up so well that at show time, he took another one. He didn't come down from his amphetamine high until the next night. "They left me exhausted, but I had discovered something I sincerely thought would be a good thing for me," Cash wrote later.[27]

He was wrong.

Late in 1957, Cash, his wife, Vivian, and their daughters, Rosanne and Kathy, moved into a brand-new and much larger house on Walnut Grove Place in Memphis. But Cash was spending more and more time in California, appearing regularly on the TV program *Town Hall Party*, which aired on Saturday nights in Los Angeles.

At *Town Hall Party*, Cash met Tex Ritter, Merle Travis, and Johnny Western. Ritter mostly recorded traditional cowboy music. Travis was best known for a recently rereleased album of folk songs (two of which, "Dark as a Dungeon" and "John Henry," Cash would make a standard part of his repertoire in the 1960s). Johnny Western, who would later join Cash's road show, specialized in Western ballads. Together, they reawakened Cash's interest in the songs of the Old West.

Meanwhile, Cash and the Tennessee Two were increasingly unhappy with Sam Phillips, even though he'd chosen to feature Cash on the first Sun Records album, *Johnny Cash with His Hot and Blue Guitar*. They thought Phillips had lost interest in Cash and was

Johnny Cash spends time with his then-wife Vivian and two of their daughters.

instead focusing his attention on what he saw as the next big thing, Jerry Lee Lewis.[28] They even suspected Sun was holding back some royalty money that should have been coming their way, though if true, that was never proved.[29]

But Cash later said his real unhappiness was with Phillips's refusal to let him record more gospel music, because Phillips couldn't make any money with gospel. "That didn't sit well with me, and when I started thinking in terms of other hard-sell music, I got more restless still," Cash wrote.[30]

Farewell to Sun

On August 31, 1957, Don Law, a producer with Columbia Records, met Cash backstage at *Town Hall Party* and asked Cash if he'd consider signing with Columbia when his Sun Records contract expired in July 1958. Cash asked if Law would let him record a gospel album. Law said he would. He said he'd be interested in talking about other hard-to-sell ideas Cash had. After further negotiations, Cash signed.

Phillips heard about it and asked Cash if it were true. Cash lied to him, and said he hadn't signed any option. "I don't know why I found it easy to lie to Sam about it, but that's how it was," he wrote.[31]

Phillips said later, "I knew when he opened his mouth he was lying. The only damn lie that Johnny Cash ever told me that I was aware of. That hurt. That *hurt*!"[32]

When Phillips found out for sure that Cash had signed the option with Columbia, he threatened to sue Columbia for contractual interference. He also insisted that Cash come back to the studio and record the rest of the songs his Sun contract required. He threatened Cash with a breach-of-contract lawsuit to make sure he complied.

Cash came into the studio in May 1958, but refused to play any of his own material. Instead he recorded some Hank Williams songs and some songs written by the engineer, Jack Clement.

On August 1, 1958, Cash's contract with Columbia Records took effect. Two weeks later he performed for

Columbia's sales representatives at their national convention in Estes Park, Colorado. They gave him a standing ovation.

With his ties to Sun Records in Memphis severed, Cash decided he should move to California. Perkins and Grant liked the idea, but they didn't stay long. The Tennessee Two moved back to Tennessee. From then on they would only reunite with Cash for concerts or recordings.

Soaring Success

The Cash family first lived in a Hollywood apartment, then moved to a new house in Encino. The family had just expanded to three with the birth of Cynthia (Cindy).

Cash's career continued to soar. As *Time* magazine noted in 1959, in just four years, songs Cash had composed had sold more than 6 million records, with "I Walk the Line" easily passing a million all on its own. "The latest, 'Don't Take Your Guns to Town,' is well on its way to repeating that performance," the magazine noted.[33]

"Don't Take Your Guns to Town" was one of the first songs Cash had recorded for Columbia. It hit just at the right time, when Westerns were wildly popular on television and in movies. The song tells the story of a young cowboy named Billie Joe who is killed in a shoot-out after he

"Don't Take Your Guns to Town" was one of the first songs Cash had recorded for Columbia.

ignores his mother's pleas to leave his guns at home. Cash had begun writing it while he was in the air force, and got the name Billy Joe from an air force buddy of his, Billy Joe Carnahan.[34]

"Don't Take Your Guns to Town" reached number one on the country charts and stayed there for six weeks. It also climbed the pop charts. Cash had eight other songs released in 1958, four of them from Columbia—and four of them from Sun Records, which still had plenty of Cash recordings tucked away.

"Don't Take Your Guns to Town" was also a featured track on Cash's first Columbia album, *The Fabulous Johnny Cash*. That was only one of three albums he released in 1959: the other two were *Hymns by Johnny Cash* (the gospel album he'd long wanted to do, recorded at last) and *Songs of Our Soil*, a collection of folk songs.

Mining the Past, Influencing the Future

The two non-gospel albums included two songs that biographer Michael Streissguth calls the "finest nuggets" Cash mined from his rural Arkansas, Great Depression past. "Pickin' Time" is a first-person song about a poor farmer hoping for better times when the harvest is done. "Five Feet High and Rising," drawn directly from the flood the Cash family experienced when Cash was five years old, is about a farmer watching floodwaters pouring over his farm.

"This choice to transform Depression stories into mass entertainment made Cash unique among the hitmakers of that time," wrote Streissguth. At a time when much of the pop music was lightweight feel-good stuff—the Beach Boys' songs about surfing and cars, the Beatles' early music—Cash was "digging up the country's thick and tangled roots."[35] That made him influential to the folksingers who would emerge in New York in the 1960s in reaction to pop.

Among those influenced was Bob Dylan, who heard Cash on the radio when he was a high school student in Hibbing, Minnesota. "It was different from anything else you had ever heard," he wrote after Cash's death. "The record sounded like a voice from the middle of the earth. It was so powerful and moving. It was profound."[36]

No other country star at the time put out three albums in a single year, but Cash still managed to keep on touring, putting together a showcase that would eventually be called *The Johnny Cash Show*. Johnny Western toured with him, and so did various female vocalists, including Rose Maddox, Patsy Cline, and, in 1962, Barbara Mandrell, who was just thirteen years old at the time.

Touring was as stressful as ever. Cash did a lot of his own driving, much to the alarm of other cast members. "He was the world's worst driver," Johnny Western remembered. "Patsy Cline wouldn't ride if he was driving."[37]

Cash needed superhuman energy to get everything done. And increasingly, he got that energy from amphetamines.

Chapter 4

Downhill Slide

Cash's addiction was well established in Memphis. It grew worse when he moved to California, which already had a thriving culture of drug use.

"My friends made a joke out of my 'nervousness,'" Cash wrote. "I had a twitch in the neck, the back, the face. My eyes dilated. I couldn't stand still. I twisted, turned, contorted, and popped my neck bones."[1]

Cash tried to keep his using secret, but at least some of his friends knew the truth. Marshall Grant figured it out early on, when he saw Cash taking pills backstage late in 1957. Even those who didn't realize Cash was on drugs couldn't ignore his increasingly erratic behavior or his weight loss. And they particularly couldn't ignore the concerts that had to be canceled because of Cash's ongoing bouts of laryngitis, a side-effect of amphetamines, which dry out the mucous membranes.

Vivian Cash knew about the pills early on. "She saw them as deadly right from the start," Cash wrote, "when she'd get up in the morning in the little house on Sandy Cove in Memphis and there I'd be, wide-awake and red-eyed after staying up all night in the den, writing and singing and putting things down on tape."[2]

But Cash didn't much care what Vivian thought. By the time he, Vivian, and the three girls moved to California in early 1959, he wrote, his marriage was "in bad trouble." Being a recording artist meant touring, which meant leaving his family. "My kids suffered—Daddy wasn't there for school plays, Fourth of July picnics . . . my absence was a loss that can never be made up."[3]

Eventually, everyone around Cash knew he was on drugs. Yet somehow he kept the shows coming. Grant recalled that sometimes he led Cash out onstage when the singer didn't even know where he was, but "lo and behold . . . he'd walk out on stage and the crowd would stand up screaming and hollering for five minutes, [and] by the time that was over with, the guy could do a show. And do a good show."[4]

Not Walking the Line

It wasn't just the drugs and the touring that ate away at the Cashes' marriage. Cash was also attracted to other women, and as a touring musician, had plenty of opportunities to pursue that attraction if he chose.

By 1960, Cash's marriage was so far gone that he didn't always bother returning to California between tours. Instead, he'd often head down to Shreveport,

Johnny Cash in the early 1960s

It wasn't just the drugs and the touring that ate away at the Cashes' marriage.

Louisiana, to spend time with his close friend Johnny Horton and Horton's wife, Billie Jean.

When Horton died in a car accident in 1960, Cash flew to Shreveport to console Billie Jean. Not long after the funeral, he flew her to New York for a three-week shopping spree, canceling concerts to do so. He told at least one person that he eventually intended to marry her.

Afterward, he kept looking after her. He arranged her finances for her, and even gave her funds from his royalties to tide her over until she got money from Horton's final hit recording, "North to Alaska."

"We were close," Billie Jean said years later, "but the only thing that put the kibosh on it was the drugs. Had he not been on the pills, trust me, I would have married him."[5]

But Cash *was* on the pills, and they kept getting him in trouble. In November 1961, Cash and another man were arrested for drunkenness at 3:30 in the morning in Nashville. Cash was attempting to kick down the door of a club. It was closed, but he thought the bouncers were just refusing to let him in.

There were troubles on the musical side of Cash's career, too. Stew Carnall became Cash's sole manager in 1961, buying out Bob Neal. But Cash soon decided Carnall wasn't much of a manager, and in July 1961, he hired a promoter from London, Ontario, Saul Holiff, who had been an unofficial advisor on Cash's frequent

Canadian tours. Holiff impressed Cash further when he managed to get an improved contract out of Columbia.

Holiff coined the phrase "America's foremost singing storyteller" to describe Cash. He booked concerts at the Hollywood Bowl and Carnegie Hall. The Carnegie Hall concert, however, proved to be a disaster. Cash had taken so much amphetamine his throat had dried out and he could barely sing.

But then Holiff did something that would eventually prove more important to Cash than any one concert could ever have been: he hired June Carter to join *The Johnny Cash Show* for a performance that December in Dallas.

Erratic Behavior

In the fall of 1961 Cash moved his family (which now included a fourth daughter, Tara) to a new home north of Ventura, California. He'd built it on fifteen acres of land halfway up a hill. It was terribly isolated for Vivian and the four girls. Rosanne Cash said "it was horrible."[6]

By that time Cash was behaving so erratically it was hard to know why he did anything he did. To his friends, he was two people in one, "one of the greatest human beings who ever walked on the face of this earth" and "the greatest jerk that ever lived," in the words of Marshall Grant.[7]

That "jerk" began showing up onstage as well as backstage. At the Grand Ole Opry in 1965, Cash lost his temper, either because he couldn't manage to free a microphone from its stand or because he found the lights too bright, and dragged the stand right across the footlights, smashing them and sending glass flying into the audience. As punishment, he was banned from the Opry.[8]

Cash had to get off drugs. Everyone knew it. But the one who finally did something about it was June Carter. She'd seen some of the same behavior from the late Hank Williams when she and the Carter Family had toured with him. She didn't want to relive the experience.

June had already been married twice by that point. In 1952 she married country star Carl Smith, with whom she had one daughter. That marriage ended in 1955. She then married a Nashville police officer, Rip Nix, in 1957, and gave birth to another daughter, Rosey. She had been limiting her touring to look after her children, but now she began spending more time on the road, both to be part of *The Johnny Cash Show* and to help look after its star.

June would hunt for Cash's pills while he was asleep and flush them down the toilet. "She once told me that if she had a dollar for every pill of Johnny Cash's that she'd flushed, none of us would ever have to work again," her son John Carter Cash wrote. "She loved him, and she wanted him to succeed—and most of all, to survive."[9]

Marshall Grant was her ally. They'd stay up all night with Cash "just to keep in touch with him, to keep him alive and stop him from hurting anybody." Neither one

of them could have succeeded by him- or herself, he
said. "We could barely do it together."[10]

Lighting the Ring of Fire

June wanted more than just to get Johnny Cash off
drugs. Increasingly, she also wanted Cash romantically.

The feeling was mutual. "Within months of meeting,
the relationship between June and Cash became a full-
blown affair," wrote Cash's authorized biographer, Steve
Turner. They kept it discreet, though. Both were still
married, and the truth would have played havoc with
Cash's public reputation as a devoted family man.[11]

While all this was going on, June was writing songs
with Merle Kilgore, who'd also written the hit song
"Wolverton Mountain," recorded by Claude King. The
first song Kilgore and June wrote together was called
"Promised to John." And then, Kilgore remembered, one
day June came to him and said she was "torn apart" and
didn't know what to do because she was so in love with
Johnny Cash.

Kilgore asked her if she had any ideas for a song, and
she told him that a friend of hers who had just gotten a
divorce had written her a letter. She read the letter to
him, and at one point it contained the phrase "I hate
love. Love is like a burning ring of fire."

Kilgore seized on that metaphor, which also seemed
to describe how June was feeling about Cash. The
resulting song, originally called "Love's Burning Ring of
Fire," was recorded by Anita Carter and released in
November 1962. Cash liked it, but told June he'd wait

four months before he did it himself, to give the original version time to succeed.[12]

By that time, Cash needed a hit himself. He hadn't had a single on the pop charts for nearly four years, and only two of his last twelve had reached the Top 100. Of all his albums, only *The Fabulous Johnny Cash* had even made the Top 20. "His records weren't selling and he was in bad shape," is how Kilgore put it. And his contract was due to expire at the end of 1963.

At Kilgore's suggestion, Cash asked his old engineer from Sun, Jack Clement, to help produce a recording of "Ring of Fire." Cash told Clement he'd had a dream about the song having trumpets in it. Trumpets were unheard of in country music at the time, but Clement went out and hired two trumpet players and told them what to play. He played guitar on the song himself.

"Ring of Fire," released in May 1963, reached number 17 on the singles charts, and a new "best-of" album, also called *Ring of Fire*, made it to number 26 in the album charts. Thanks to that success, Cash's Columbia contract was renewed.

Johnny and June

Cash and June Carter recorded "The Legend of John Henry's Hammer" together in June 1962. Later that month they recorded the first song they cowrote, "The Matador." A few weeks after that, Cash was a special guest for a day at a Carter Family recording session.

By June 1962 Vivian Cash had realized something was going on. She had brought the children and Cash's parents, Ray and Carrie, to Cash's Hollywood Bowl show. Afterward they went backstage, and, Kathy Cash remembered, "We were standing there waving good-bye to Dad, and he kissed us all, got into his car, and then June [with Luther and Marshall] jumped into the car right next to him and waved to us. Mom was furious . . . That was when she started falling apart."[13]

> **Cash thought June understood him just fine. He also saw her as a steadying influence.**

On the rare occasions when her father came home, Kathy would lie awake at night listening to her parents fight. Vivian wanted a husband who was home more often, and mentally and physically present when he was home. Cash felt so misunderstood by her that he recorded a song called "Understand Your Man" in February 1964, obviously directed at Vivian.

Cash thought June understood him just fine. He also saw her as a steadying influence. She didn't drink, she didn't do drugs, and she was trying to stop him from doing them, too.

A Foray Into Folk

Cash also liked the connection he had through June Carter to the Carter Family, who were legends in the folk-music community. Folk music was about to get its own taste of the spotlight as young people, turned off by the commercialism and slickness of commercial pop, turned to it for a taste of "authenticity."

Cash's interest in folk took him to New York City, which had a thriving folk music scene. There he met Peter La Farge, who in 1961 had recorded "The Ballad of Ira Hayes." The song tells the story of Ira Hamilton Hayes, a Pima Indian who was one of the six marines in the famous photograph of the American flag being raised on the island of Iwo Jima during the Second World War. Hayes died a poverty-stricken alcoholic in 1955. The song pointed out that even though Hayes had fought for his country, his ancestral land did not have enough water.

Cash recorded the song in March 1964. It was the first flat-out protest song he had ever recorded. Some country music DJs even refused to play it because they considered it too controversial. Cash went on to build a whole concept album, called *Bitter Tears*, around the plight of American Indians. The *New York Times* praised it as "one of the best LPs to emerge from the '60s folk movement."[14]

Cash also sang "The Ballad of Ira Hayes" at the Newport Folk Festival on July 26, 1964. He'd been exchanging letters with Bob Dylan off and on, and at Newport they finally met up and spent a night taping songs in a local motel with Joan Baez and her sister and brother-in-law, Mimi and Richard Farina. Two days later Cash and his band recorded a first take of Dylan's "Mama You've Been on My Mind." Later that summer, Cash and June recorded Dylan's "It Ain't Me Babe," which made it to the top five of the country charts and crossed over to the pop charts, too.

Cash's interest in folk music was very apparent over the next year in his choice of music. He not only recorded other people's folk songs, but he also wrote his own protest song, "All of God's Children Ain't Free." Another folk song, "Orange Blossom Special," scaled both the country and pop chart. For his next album, Cash recorded the two-disc *Johnny Cash Sings Ballads of the True West*. It was too expensive for most buyers, but a single-disc version released in 1966 reached number 4 on the country charts.

But while all this apparent success was going on in his public life, in his personal life, Johnny Cash was about to reach rock bottom . . . and start the long climb back up.

Chapter 5

Clean and Sober

Late in September 1965, Cash was supposed to be part of a "Nashville in New York" edition of CBS-TV's *Steve Lawrence Show*. He and the Tennessee Three (they'd expanded from the Tennessee Two in 1960 with the addition of drummer W. S. "Fluke" Holland) were supposed to open the finale with "I Walk the Line." Cash, strung out on drugs, was unable to perform, and was pulled from the show.

Cash's troupe headed south for a short tour of Texas. After the last show in Dallas, Cash didn't take the flight he was booked on to Los Angeles. Instead he went to El Paso. From there he took a cab to Juarez, Mexico. And there, he bought socks stuffed with amphetamines.

On October 4, while he waited on a plane at El Paso International Airport, he was arrested by two narcotics agents. They thought he'd bought heroin in Juarez. He hadn't, but it was just as illegal to buy amphetamines, so Cash was thrown in jail. The wire services soon

Johnny Cash, center, is escorted to a federal courthouse in Texas in October 1965.

picked up on the arrest. When reporters gathered in the courtroom for his bond hearing, Cash snarled at them and threatened to kick one photographer's camera right out of his hands.

Cash later called the press coverage the "public documentation of the low point of my entire career." He stayed clean and sober for six weeks, but as his demanding tour schedule heated up, he wrote, "I returned once again to my shadows of death—the pills."[1]

"Two weeks after he started again, he was back in, head over heels, worse than ever," Marshall Grant recalled.[2]

Two months after being released from jail, Cash was back in El Paso for his arraignment. He pleaded guilty to possession of illegal drugs. The charge carried a maximum sentence of a thousand-dollar fine, one year in prison, or both.

Once he was back on the pills, Cash behaved as erratically as ever. In March 1966, with three thousand people in the audience, he wandered barefoot onstage at Toronto's O'Keefe Centre, in Holiff's words, "very, very, very strung out." Holiff brought down the curtain and canceled the show.[3]

In May, Cash flew to London for a tour of the British Isles. He met up again with Bob Dylan, who was also on tour, and attended one of his shows. Holiff, with a great deal of difficult negotiation, had lined up a prestigious show for Cash at the Olympia Theatre in Paris. The performance was supposed to immediately follow the British tour, but Cash didn't show up at the airport for the flight to France. He couldn't: he had been partying too hard with Dylan. Furious, Holiff flew back to the United States.

When Cash returned to the United States, he went home briefly, then headed off on yet another tour. When that one was over, he didn't go home at all. Instead, he stayed with his friend Gene Ferguson in Brentwood, California. Both Vivian and June Carter kept calling

Ferguson to see if Cash was there. At Cash's request, Ferguson lied to both of them and said he wasn't.[4]

The Divorce

Vivian had had enough. On June 30, 1966, she filed for divorce. She cited "extreme cruelty" and "grievous mental suffering and anguish." She was worried that Cash would sell their communal property or try to conceal some of his earnings. She wanted a share of both for child support, so she requested and received a court order to prevent him from doing either. Since she didn't know where he was, she had the court order published four times in the *Nashville Banner* in August 1966. Cash was ordered to appear in court on August 22 in Ventura, California.

Cash didn't show up. On August 29 his attorney responded to the complaint. He denied that Cash had shown extreme cruelty, inflicted grievous mental suffering, or had any intention of concealing his wealth or disposing of any property.

Negotiations continued. Kathy Cash asked her mother what it would mean if she and Cash got a divorce. Vivian told her not to worry because the only difference would be that "Daddy's clothes would no longer be hanging in the closet."[5]

On August 30, 1967, after more than a year, Cash finally quit fighting the divorce. Vivian received custody of the children, a guarantee of four hundred dollars a month, plus medical care and insurance, per child,

A concert poster from the mid-1960s.

sixty-five hundred dollars to pay her attorney's fee, and a substantial financial settlement.[6]

As the divorce proceedings wound down, Cash decided to buy a new house overlooking Old Hickory Lake in Hendersonville, Tennessee, north of Nashville. He would live there for the rest of his life.

Trying to Go Straight

Cash desperately wanted—or said he wanted—to kick his drug habit once and for all. But he didn't seem to be able to manage it. Marshall Grant estimates that by 1967 fully half of Cash's shows were being canceled, causing immense problems for Holiff. Promoters knew how many Cash concerts were falling through, and didn't want to book him. Holiff sent a telegram to Cash that read, "Your professional behavior is totally reprehensible, showing a complete disregard for the rights and feelings of every one around you."[7]

> Cash desperately wanted—or said he wanted—to kick his drug habit once and for all.

But what finally convinced Cash to get off drugs wasn't his habit's impact on his career, but its impact on his love life. With his divorce final, he could finally marry June Carter, if she'd have him. He'd asked her many times over the years, and she'd always put him off. Now, at last, she said yes, but she set one condition: he had to kick his drug habit.

Over the years Cash told different stories about how he finally reached a turn-around point. In his 1997 autobiography, and in other interviews in the 1990s, he said he walked into Nickajack Cave (now flooded by the waters of Nickajack Lake) near Chattanooga with every intention of getting lost in it and starving to death. Instead, he said, he felt a "great comfortin' presence" telling him that he wasn't going to die, that "I got things for you to do." He also said that June and his mother were waiting for him when he reached daylight, and drove him back to Nashville, and that on the way back he told them he was ready to recommit his life to God and kick his drug habit.[8]

"That did not happen," according to Marshall Grant.[9]

Cash himself didn't mention any attempted suicide in a cave in his first autobiography, published in 1975. There, he puts the turning point on the night he spent in jail in Lafayette, Georgia, in November 1967.

The sheriff, Ralph Jones, had Cash picked up after he knocked on the wrong door in the middle of the night, frightening the woman who lived there. Rather than charge Cash with disorderly conduct, he asked Cash why he would throw away his career, his family, and everything he'd earned for the sake of getting stoned on pills. "I just felt led to say that to him," he said later.[10]

Cash wrote that he went out, got in the car where a friend, Richard McGibony, was waiting, and said, "You'll never see me high on dope any more."[11]

For whatever reason, he agreed, at June's urging, to meet with psychiatrist Nat Winston. Cash told Winston he'd been taking twenty or thirty amphetamine capsules at a time, three or four times a day, then taking twenty or so tranquilizers a night to try to get some rest. "He was indeed quite ill," Winston said, in what sounds like a considerable understatement.[12]

One-on-one counseling and a concerted effort to keep the pills away from Cash followed, but Cash would struggle with drugs for the rest of his life.

> "My liberation from drug addiction wasn't permanent," Cash wrote in 1997.

"My liberation from drug addiction wasn't permanent," he wrote in 1997. "Though I've never regressed to spending years at a time on amphetamines, I've used mood-altering drugs at various lengths of times since 1967: amphetamines, sleeping pills, and prescription painkillers."[13]

Marshall Grant was considerably blunter: "There wasn't five days from 1976 until he came down with his disease that he was straight," he claimed.[14]

Still, some kind of corner had been turned. On November 11, 1967, Cash performed a benefit concert for Hendersonville High School to raise money for new band uniforms. It was the first time he had performed drug-free in more than a decade. "I was terrified," he wrote; but he discovered that being onstage without the benefit of drugs was not as frightening as he'd thought. Relaxed, joking with the audience, he amazed himself.[15]

And then, in January 1968, came the live recording at Folsom Prison.

Things Start Looking Up

Johnny Cash at Folsom Prison hit at the perfect time. It didn't sound like anything else out there. It was alternative, and by that point of the tumultuous 1960s, alternative was good. So was "antiestablishment," anything that pushed back against conventional society. What could be more antiestablishment than an album recorded in a prison?

The result, according to critic Greg Kot, "isn't just one of Cash's best albums, it's one of the best live albums ever made and a country music landmark."[16]

"Nobody else in popular music could match Cash for radical nerve or compassion," wrote *Rolling Stone*'s Mikal Gilmore.[17]

The turnaround in Cash's life carried on through the rest of the year. On February 22, 1968, the newly divorced Cash proposed to June Carter on-stage in London, Ontario. They were married just a little over a week later, at the Methodist Church in Franklin, Kentucky. In between the proposal and the marriage, they stopped off in Hollywood to collect a Grammy Award for best country and western performance by a duo for "Jackson."

Cash had also rededicated himself to his religious beliefs. "God had done more than speak to me," he wrote in his 1997 autobiography. "He had revealed His will to me through other people, family and friends. The greatest joy of my life was that I no longer felt separated from Him."[18]

His religious reawakening inspired his next album after the Folsom Prison recording. *The Holy Land* combined new gospel songs with comments and thoughts Cash and June recorded as they toured Israel shortly after their marriage.

Not everything that happened in 1968 was good, though. In early August, Luther Perkins, Cash's longtime guitar player and one of the original members of the Tennessee Two, fell asleep on his sofa in Hendersonville. He had a lit cigarette in his hand. The sofa ignited. Perkins died of his burns two days later.

Cash felt guilty. Perkins had asked him to come over and Cash had refused. Not only that, Perkins had been drunk when the accident occurred, and Cash felt responsible for contributing to his chemical abuse. "A part of me died with Luther," Cash told an interviewer ten years later.[19]

Carl Perkins filled in for Luther Perkins for a few shows, but then one night when Cash was playing in Fayetteville, Arkansas, Carl wasn't there because his flight had been delayed. In the audience was a guitarist from Tulsa named Bob Wootton, who had memorized the guitar part on every Johnny Cash recording up until then and had made the trip because he wanted to see Cash in person. He was pulled from the audience to fill in, while a local bass player filled in on bass. Nobody remembers the bass player, but Bob Wootton would play with Cash for most of the next thirty years.[20]

In 1968, Johnny Cash and June Carter wed.

"A Boy Named Sue"

In early 1969, Cash recorded his second prison album, *Johnny Cash at San Quentin*. This one was filmed by the U.K.'s Granada Television for a documentary. It featured the song "A Boy Named Sue," written by Shel Silverstein, best known now as the author and illustrator of children's poetry books such as *Where the Sidewalk Ends*. "A Boy Named Sue" was the first single released from the album, and it reached number 2 on the singles charts—Cash's best position ever. Of course he appreciated the success, but he was a little annoyed, too. He would have preferred to have his most popular song be one that he wrote.[21]

There was a scary moment near the end of the concert. The inmates were standing on the tables, screaming, after Cash played "San Quentin" as an encore. The guards were nervous. Everyone was nervous. Ralph Gleason, a concert reviewer for *Rolling Stone*, said, "If he had screwed up one notch higher the joint would have exploded."[22] But Cash took a moment to calm things down, then played a less aggressive version of the song. He would later claim, though, that in the heat of the moment, he was tempted to say "Let's do it" and unleash a riot.[23]

Johnny Cash at San Quentin was even more popular than the Folsom Prison recording, not only because of "A Boy Named Sue" but also because of something else boosting Cash's popularity at the time: his own network television show.

The Johnny Cash Show

The Granada Television documentary, which aired in
Britain during April 1969, before the San Quentin album
was released, may have helped ABC-TV realize how
charismatic a performer Cash could be. They asked him
to host his own network television show as a summer
replacement for *Hollywood Palace*. Holiff agreed, provided
Cash could film the shows in Nashville's Ryman
Auditorium (home of the Grand Ole Opry). He also
insisted that the producer would be Stan Jacobson, who
had made a 1967 TV special that had aired on CBC-TV in
Canada. ABC said yes, and filming began in April 1969.

Although Cash had come a long way, he was still
battling drugs. The difference, according to Marshall
Grant, was that he had it under control. "Any time he
wanted to come back down he could do it. He'd do what
he needed to do." He put on weight, and by the time the
show started filming, he "looked excellent."[24]

The show rehearsed Mondays, Tuesdays, and
Wednesdays. Tapings (usually two shows a week) were
on Thursdays. Cash continued to perform concerts on
the weekends.

Cash claimed he'd never liked television, but now, he
said, "I have decided I am going to like it. I mean, if I'm
going to have to do it every day, I might as well enjoy
it." Even though he didn't like being "confined," he
said, "I like my guests."[25]

Those guests made *The Johnny Cash Show*,
particularly its early episodes, different from everything

Bono's First Taste of Cash

Among the viewers Cash impressed was a nine-year-old boy in Ireland named Paul David Hewson. Years later, the world would know him as Bono, lead singer for the band U2.

Looking back, Bono called *The Johnny Cash Show* "an amazingly generous act, a great gift to the world," that moved people like Dylan from the fringe to the center of the entertainment world.[26]

Twenty-five years later, Bono would be instrumental in launching Cash's final amazing career comeback, helping move *him* back "from the fringe to the center of the entertainment world."

else on television. Cash wanted to showcase talented performers viewers had rarely seen. His opening show featured Bob Dylan and Joni Mitchell. Later guests that first summer included Merle Haggard, Buffy Saint-Marie, Mama Cass, Gordon Lightfoot, and Linda Ronstadt. None of them was as famous then as they would become, and all were from the folk, blues, or country worlds, rather than pop.

Cash soon ran afoul of the conservative network bosses. He wanted to have Pete Seeger as a guest, but Seeger was both a former Communist and an antiwar activist. "Pete Seeger is a great American," he complained to the director, Bill Carruthers. "Why can't I have my friends on his show?"[27] Eventually the network relented.

But in exchange, Cash also had to have on some of the guests who showed up on every variety show of the period: Bob Hope, Phil Harris, and others whose style of entertainment had little to do with his own.

Summer replacement shows usually lasted just one summer. But the popularity of the *Johnny Cash at San Quentin* album prompted a lot of people to tune in, and they liked what they saw. ABC picked up the show for seventeen more episodes, beginning in January 1970.

In each show Cash sang some of his well-known songs solo, sang duets with guests and with June, and finished with a gospel song with the Carter Family and the Statler Brothers. In the second season, more top-notch musical guests showed up, including Ray Charles, Judy Collins, Roy Orbison, Roger Miller, and Waylon Jennings.

A filmed section in the middle of the show, called "Ride This Train," focused on some aspect of American life or history. Topics included religion, prisons, hoboes, cotton picking, trains, and the Wild West. Cash, often in period costume, would talk directly to the camera about the topic. It became Cash's favorite part of the show and helped establish him as someone who preserved American traditions and stories.

A successful network program also helped people forget about the Johnny Cash who had been in the headlines just a year or two before, the one who missed shows, broke footlights, and got arrested for possession of illegal drugs.

Kris Kristofferson appeared on the show in 1970. "By the time he did his TV show he was such a figure of stability," he said. "It was like he was the father of our country."[28]

Cash might not have been the father of the country, but he was the father of a new son: John Carter, his only child with June Carter, born in March 1970. With the birth of his son, Cash finally got off drugs completely.

His lifelong spiritual quest continued. He befriended evangelist Billy Graham, and appeared with the Carter Family and the Statler Brothers at a Billy Graham youth revival in Knoxville, Tennessee, on May 24, 1970. He talked about his drug abuse. "It ain't worth it," he said. He later called the appearance with Graham "the pinnacle of my career."[29]

"The Man in Black"

One song written just for *The Johnny Cash Show* was "Man in Black." Cash had been wearing mostly black outfits on stage for years. When asked why, he'd given three different reasons.

One reason, he said, was that black stayed cleanest longest, an important consideration during long road trips.

Another reason he sometimes gave was that he wore it because black was good for wearing in church, where his first concert had been.

Sometimes he said that black was simply easier to coordinate.

But in "Man in Black," he endowed his choice in clothes with greater significance, saying that he'd made that somber choice in remembrance of sorrow and injustice.

"The Man in Black" became one of Cash's well-known nicknames.

Religion and TV Don't Mix

After the second season aired, the show was renewed for a full year, twenty-six episodes, starting in September 1970. But in the show that aired on November 18, 1970, Cash made an explicit statement about his Christian belief.

Producer Stan Jacobson had warned him not to do it. He told Cash it would alienate a segment of his audience. But Cash insisted.

In his second autobiography, Cash wrote that he knew Jacobson was right, but that he had to "let the chips fall where they may." He said he'd been getting thousands of letters from people asking him if he was a Christian, and he felt he had to take a stand.[30]

"After that statement, the show took a nose dive," Jacobson said. The network began trying stunts to boost the ratings, even making Cash do a mini-special at a circus. The program ended for good in March 1971. Cash heard the news while he was touring in Australia. NBC invited him to move the show to their network, but Cash refused. After the initial shock of the cancellation, he seemed more relieved than anything else.[31]

"Television steals your soul," he told one reporter.[32]

Although admitting that the "worldly consequences" of his decision to explicitly talk about his faith on his show "were severe," Cash wrote that he never regretted speaking up. "You have to admit that if you were in my shoes and believed what I believe, you'd have been a

In 1971, Johnny Cash and Kirk Douglas appeared in the movie *A Gunfight*.

fool to choose a decade or two's worth of record sales over eternal salvation."[33]

Johnny Cash was an international celebrity now, famous around the world. He'd appeared in a movie with Kirk Douglas, a western called *A Gunfight*. He had a new son. He made an estimated $3 million a year and had a beautiful home surrounded by 146 acres of land. He had a newfound commitment to his faith, and he was clean of drugs.

But, as always with Cash, from one of the high points of his career there was only one way to go: down.

The Low Point

The decline in Cash's career was gradual. Clean of drugs, with a new baby boy and money rolling in, he seemed to have it made.

The fact that his forthright proclamation of his Christian faith on his TV show may have contributed to its cancellation didn't worry Cash. He'd always included gospel numbers on the show and in his concerts. Now he focused even more strongly on his religious convictions.

On May 9, 1971, Cash answered the altar call at Evangel Temple, an Assembly of God church in Madison, Tennessee. The preacher was Jimmy Snow, son of country music legend Hank Snow. Snow, who had made it his mission to have a Christian impact on country music, later said, "It is one thing for a public figure to join a church. It is another thing for him to humble himself enough to get down on his knees and crawl and cry in front of a congregation."[1]

"I don't have a career anymore," Cash said. "What I have now is a ministry."[2]

With Cash's new religious commitment came a spate of religion-themed projects. Chief among them was *Gospel Road*, a ninety-minute movie about Jesus's life. *Gospel Road* was filmed in Israel through November 1971. It was directed by Robert Elfstrom, who also portrayed Jesus. June played Mary Magdalene. Reba Hancock, Cash's sister, played the Virgin Mary. Jimmy Snow played Pontius Pilate and Saul Holiff played the high priest Caiphas. A group of European backpackers played the twelve apostles.

A year of editing followed. Cash added his own songs and songs by others, including Larry Gatlin, Kris Kristofferson, and John Denver.

> "I don't have a career anymore," Cash said. "What I have now is a ministry."

But though *Gospel Road* was obviously a labor of love and faith for Cash, it didn't make much of a splash in movie theaters, even though it got a lot of media attention and a very positive review in *Newsweek*. The associated album made it only to number 12 on the country charts, the worst performance of any Cash album up until that point. The only single released from it, "Children," only made it to number 30.

Biographer Michael Streissguth, however, praises Cash for the effort. "Few, if any of his peers had stepped from their regular recording careers to pursue a new genre, and the fact that Cash did so is a tribute to his continued desire to challenge himself by reaching for new spheres," he writes.

Cash called it "the most ambitious project I've ever attempted."[3]

Unfortunately, Streissguth notes, the movie "receded into the background of Cash's career because America's arbiters of chic rejected it."[4] *Rolling Stone* ran an extensive profile of Cash after the movie came out, but made no mention of either it or the associated album.[5]

Religious Concerts

Cash continued his secular concerts, but he also did more and more religious concerts. He played for Explo '72 (the name was a play on Expo, for exposition, and explosion, as in "youth explosion"), sponsored by Campus Crusade for Christ. It drew 80,000 young people to Dallas, and more than 150,000 people attended the closing concert at an abandoned racetrack. Billy Graham, a keynote speaker, called it a "religious Woodstock."[6]

Cash was in London for a similar event in 1973 at Wembley Stadium. He also played on the *Grand Ole Gospel Hour*, created by Jimmy Snow. Modeled on the Grand Ole Opry, it took place in Nashville's Ryman Auditorium after the Opry show. He performed for other evangelists, including Oral Roberts.

His personal story as a man who had come back from drug addiction and brushes with the law to rebuild his career and proclaim the Good News enhanced his reputation with mainstream America. He was asked to perform at the White House by President Richard Nixon. He was friends with Billy and Ruth Graham. He made frequent television appearances, not just as a singer, but as an actor: for instance, he played a dishonest evangelist on NBC-TV's detective show *Columbo*.

But despite all that activity, his record sales kept falling. *The Gospel Road* hadn't done well. *The Junkie and the Juicehead Minus Me*, which featured a lot of the aspiring singers in his family (including June's daughters Carlene Smith and Rosey Nix and Cash's daughter Rosanne) did even worse in 1974. Neither of its two singles made it onto the country charts.

Columbia asked Cash to record an album of new songs by young songwriters, but when it came out in 1975, it was a failure. Only "The Lady Came From Baltimore," written by Tim Hardin, made it onto the country charts, topping out at number 14. Although that was Cash's best showing in two years, the other songs simply weren't well suited to Cash's style of singing. His most powerful numbers had always been the ones he wrote himself, but he wasn't writing anymore.

More Mainstream, Less Popular

Cash's mainstream success may actually have contributed to his decline as a recording artist and songwriter. Fans in the 1960s had been drawn to his rebelliousness, highlighted in his prison concerts. Now he was meeting with President Nixon and hanging out

In March 1976, Johnny Cash was awarded a star on the Hollywood Walk of Fame in Los Angeles, California. With him are his wife June Carter and their son John.

with Billy Graham. He wasn't "alternative" or "countercultural" anymore.

"He used to write a lot of good songs before he started hanging out with the wrong company there at the White House," was how folksinger Phil Ochs put it. Waylon Jennings said Cash had "sold out to religion."[7]

Proof of his mainstream appeal was the fact that he was recruited for many of the celebrations surrounding the United States Bicentennial (200th anniversary) in 1976. Cash had always been interested in American history. He'd already released, back in 1972, a concept album entitled *America: A 200-Year Salute in Story and Song*. He'd also made a 1974 TV special called *Ridin' The Rails*, the story of the building of the country through the building of the railroad.

Shortly after *America* came out, Saul Holiff retired as Cash's manager and Lou Robin took over. Holiff said it was entirely voluntary. Even though Cash seemed to be at the peak of the business, Holiff said, "I truly believed that it was going to be anticlimactic from then onward, and it was. For the next ten or twelve years he went into a tailspin."[8]

That tailspin didn't exactly manifest itself right away, though. The bicentennial celebrations kept Cash in the spotlight. He hosted a TV special and a four-episode run of *The New Johnny Cash Show*. He received a star on Hollywood Boulevard, and on July 4 was Grand Marshall for the Bicentennial Parade in Washington, D.C., which included a concert in front of the Washington Monument.

His 1976 album, *One Piece at a Time*, featured a title track that was his biggest hit in years, eventually reaching number one on the country charts. It even made the Top 40 charts, though it stalled at 29.

But Cash continued to worry about his album sales. He talked about doing an album based on his old Sun Records days, with songs by Elvis Presley, Carl Perkins, and Roy Orbison. But it never happened. Instead he recorded *The Rambler*. Based on old-time radio shows, it told the story of a man wandering the highways. It flopped.

Back on Drugs, Worse Than Ever

Cash had other problems. According to Marshall Grant, by 1976 he was back on drugs, worse than ever.[9] By 1977, he'd stopped attending Evangel Temple, and switched to the Hendersonville Church of God. After another year and a half he stopped going there, too. Oddly enough, though, at about the same time, in May 1977, he received an associate of theology degree for having successfully finished an intensive Bible-study correspondence course with the Christian International School of Theology. He was a straight-A student. He also continued performing at Billy Graham rallies.

His 1978 album *Golden Girl* didn't even make the country charts. And people he knew from his early years in the business were beginning to die. His old rival Elvis Presley, for example, died on August 16, 1977. Presley's autopsy revealed eleven different drugs in his bloodstream. It should have served as a wake-up call to Cash about his own drug use—but it didn't.

June Carter's mother, Mother Maybelle Carter, died on October 23, 1978. Sara Carter, the last living member of the original Carter Family, died three months later.

In 1979, Columbia released an album called *Silver*, celebrating Cash's twenty-fifth anniversary. It was really released a year early, probably in the hope it would drive up record sales. In 1980, his real twenty-fifth anniversary year, Cash brought out an album called *Rockabilly Blues*. Both contained excellent work. Neither made much of a splash.

End of the Tennessee Two

Silver was the last album featuring Marshall Grant, the only remaining member of the original Tennessee Two. Cash seems to have thought Grant was too controlling, and was fed up with Grant's efforts to keep him off of drugs. But Marshall was equally fed up with Cash. He called the last few years with Cash, after he was back on drugs, "a living hell."[10]

"There was no excuse for it," he said. "I'm seventy-five years old and I've never tasted a drop of alcohol . . . that's the proof you can do it if you have the fortitude." According to Grant, he was told that after he left the show Cash got even wilder. "June couldn't do anything with him and no one else cared."[11]

The two men exchanged strongly worded letters. In June 1981 Grant filed a $2.6 million lawsuit, charging Cash with breach of contract and slander. About the same time, relatives of Luther Perkins also claimed his estate was owed money. Eventually the case was settled out of court.

According to Grant, near the end of Cash's life, the two men reconciled.[12]

Cash kept struggling musically. Changes in the music industry were favoring younger artists. New stars on the country scene were making more money than he was, and attracting the hot new songwriters. He kept recording, but the hits weren't coming.

In an attempt to rejuvenate his career, Cash surrounded himself with younger producers and musicians, including his own daughter Rosanne, whose album *Seven Year Ache* had gone gold, and June's daughter Carlene. Carlene had married British musician Nick Lowe, who had been central to the New Wave in pop music. He'd produced Elvis Costello's first five albums and formed the band Rockpile with Dave Edmunds.

> **"Sometimes in the early '80s I really cared about recording, but sometimes I didn't. . . ."**

But despite all of that, as Cash himself said in his second autobiography, "Sometimes in the early '80s I really cared about recording, but sometimes I didn't. . . . Periodically, someone took the initiative and suggested something new or different to turn the situation around, but nothing ever worked."[13]

He was still touring successfully, and in 1981 he appeared in the critically acclaimed CBS-TV movie

The Pride of Jessi Hallam, a film about adult illiteracy. But he knew he was simply riding on the coattails of his own previous success. His stage show during this time featured a new ensemble he called the Great Eighties Eight, which included horns and a synthesizer—a far cry from the stripped-down sound Cash had made his name with when he performed with the Tennessee Two.

Attacked by an Ostrich

Cash's musical struggles were made worse by his perennial battle with drugs. After eye surgery in 1981, he took the painkillers the doctors prescribed. He kept right on taking them after he didn't need them anymore. His abuse of them grew even worse after a bizarre incident in September 1981. While he was walking through his personal animal park, across the street from his house in Hendersonville, he was attacked by an ostrich.

"Waldo" may have been upset because his mate had just died. His attack broke two of Cash's lower ribs and ripped his abdomen open. "If the belt hadn't been good and strong, with a solid buckle, he'd have spilled my guts exactly the way he meant to," Cash wrote later. Cash broke three more ribs when he fell on a rock.

Cash liked the way painkillers made him feel. He started seeking out multiple doctors to get the amount of painkillers he needed to feed his new habit. When the painkillers started upsetting his digestive system, he started drinking wine, which also took the edge off of the amphetamines he'd resumed taking.

Johnny Cash in 1982

The result, as he put it, was that he was "up and running, strung out, slowed down, sped up, turned around, hung on the hook, having a ball, living in hell."[14]

As if that wasn't enough, while he and June, their son John Carter (eleven years old at the time), and other guests were at Cash's vacation house in Jamaica, Cinnamon Hill, over Christmas in 1981, three men wearing stockings over their heads, armed with a machete, a knife, and a gun, broke in. The family was held hostage for four hours before the robbers fled in June's Land Rover with about fifty thousand dollars worth of stolen goods.

The thieves were soon caught. Two were jailed and later died trying to escape. The third was killed while resisting arrest. Jamaican Prime Minister Edward Seaga personally apologized to the Cashes.

On November 10, 1983, Cash's new personal cocktail of painkillers, amphetamines, tranquilizers, and liquor caught up with him. In Nottingham, England, near the end of a European tour, he decided that the old hotel they were staying in had a fold-up bed in the wall. It didn't. Nevertheless, he tried to tear the wall apart with his bare hands. He drove splinters into his right hand, which became so badly infected that when he returned to Nashville, it had to be operated on. While he was in the

> On November 10, 1983, Cash's new personal cocktail of painkillers, amphetamines, tranquilizers, and liquor caught up with him.

hospital, the doctors discovered he was also suffering from internal bleeding. More surgery was performed to remove his damaged duodenum and part of his spleen, stomach, and intestines. Cash had taken his own stock of drugs into the hospital with him, but post-surgery they also put him on morphine, which made him suffer intense hallucinations.[15]

His family took the opportunity to arrange for Cash to be admitted to the Betty Ford Center, a drug addiction treatment center in Rancho Mirage, California. When he emerged after forty-three days, his friends saw an enormous change. He was "so sober and lucid all the time," said Karen Robin, wife of manager Lou Robin.[16]

It didn't last. "Now I know where to go to get help," Cash wrote in his second autobiography in 1997, but "I've gone and got it several times since that first awakening . . . because my problem persists."[17]

The Highwaymen

The next year, 1984, Cash wrapped up another European tour with a Christmas special in Montreaux, Switzerland. Waylon Jennings, Willie Nelson, Kris Kristofferson, Toni Wine, Connie Nelson, and Jessi Colter were his special guests. Out of that special came a country music "supergroup" called the Highwaymen, who got their name from a 1977 song by Jimmy Webb. Impromptu recording sessions back in the United States produced a ten-song album of the same name.

"Highwayman" (the song) made it to number one, as did *Highwaymen* (the album) in 1985. The group toured

Cash and His Father

Cash's father, Ray Cash, died on December 23, 1985. Cash had taken good care of his parents over the years. He'd moved them into a house near his own near Hendersonville. He often praised his father in concerts. He never talked about the violence or verbal abuse Ray Cash had inflicted on his family. He always dedicated the song "These Hands" to his father.

But in his 1997 autobiography, Cash wrote that whenever he made that dedication, to the parents who worked so hard to put him through school and encouraged him to go out and sing, he could hear his father's presence protesting, "I didn't encourage you."

"He was right, of course," Cash wrote. "His attitude had always been, 'You won't amount to a hill of beans.'"[18]

"He never once told me he loved me . . . It would have meant an awful lot for me to have heard it, just once, before he died."[19]

together several times and made two more recordings, but never recaptured that initial success.

Despite the success of the Highwaymen, Cash's solo efforts went nowhere. Work on his own album, *Rainbow*, was held up for *Highwaymen*, and then for an album of duets with Waylon Jennings. In the meantime, Cash finally returned to Sun Records for *The Class of '55*, which also featured Carl Perkins, Roy Orbison, and Jerry Lee Lewis. It was released by Polygram, not Cash's own label Columbia.

When *Rainbow* finally came out, neither it nor any of its tracks made it onto the charts. According to Cash's

In 1985, the Highwaymen performed in Nashville, Tennessee. From left to right: Willie Nelson, Kris Kristofferson, Waylon Jennings, and Johnny Cash.

manager, Lou Robin, "Columbia buried it," giving it no promotion.[20]

The fact was, Columbia no longer believed Cash was worth much as a solo artist. His contract with the company expired in the spring of 1986, and on July 16, 1986, the *Nashville Tennessean* newspaper reported that Columbia would not be renewing it. After twenty-eight years, Johnny Cash was no longer a Columbia recording artist.[21]

On August 21, 1986, Cash signed a new contract with Polygram to record on its Mercury label. His first album for Mercury was *Johnny Cash Is Coming to Town*.

"The Chicken in Black"

One of the worst songs Cash ever recorded was also one of the last singles he recorded for Columbia. It was called "The Chicken in Black." For the video, he dressed up in a superhero blue cape, yellow jersey, and tights.

"It was intentionally atrocious," Cash claims in his second autobiography. "I was burlesquing myself and forcing CBS to go along with it."[22]

That's not quite the story he told *Musician* magazine in 1988. There he said he'd hated the song from the first day. He refused to admit he even knew the words anymore. "It was an embarrassment," he said.[23]

It reunited him with Jack Clement, who had worked with Cash on and off over the years since the Sun Records days. Mercury promoted *Johnny Cash Is Coming to Town* as Cash's comeback album, but though it did better than Cash's most recent previous albums, neither it nor its two singles made much of an impact on the charts.

Next up was an album of duets, *Water from the Wells of Home*. It did even worse.

And then, in 1988, Cash's health crashed again. He needed bypass surgery to replace blocked arteries around his heart. After the surgery, he contracted pneumonia. He wasn't able to perform again until March 1989, and in May he was back in a hospital in Paris, France, with chest pain. Throat problems plagued him over the next few months, and just before Thanksgiving, he checked into another drug treatment center.

His struggles weren't over. In January 1990 a dentist removed an abscessed tooth. A cyst developed that had to be scraped away. In March, he broke his jaw, which had been weakened by the surgery. The additional surgery to fix it left the bottom half of his face disfigured, and damaged the nerve endings around the bone. He'd live the rest of his life with the pain, which he sometimes compared to a blowtorch being held to his jaw.

Record troubles, drug troubles, injuries, surgeries—the 1980s were probably the lowest of all decades for Johnny Cash. His health problems could have spelled the end of his career, but they didn't.

No one knew it in 1990, of course, but Johnny Cash was just a few years away from the most remarkable comeback of them all.

Chapter 7

The Final Comeback

Cash's mother, Carrie, died on March 11, 1991, at the age of eighty-six. According to Cash biographer Steve Turner, Carrie Cash was "the biggest single influence on his life," not only encouraging him in his music career but also in his Christian faith. She had been the one who told him his voice was a gift from God. After her death, Cash cried publicly for the first time anyone could remember.[1]

Cash himself had already been very close to death. Touring had become much more difficult, and his concerts in the United States were no longer drawing sell-out crowds (though people still flocked to see him Europe). That may have been one reason he decided to set up shop in Branson, Missouri.

Branson was full of theaters where other fading and/or aging country stars had taken to performing regularly for the tourists who flocked to see them. Cash agreed to lend his name to Cash Country, which was being designed and built by David Green, a California property developer. The plan was that Cash would perform seventy-five nights a year in one of the planned $35 million entertainment complex's three 2,500-seat theaters.

Cash Country was also supposed to include, within its one hundred acres, a horse arena, a go-cart track, an amusement park, a water park, a museum (modeled on the existing Johnny Cash Museum in Hendersonville, which had opened in 1979), a hotel, three motels, and a shopping mall. It was supposed to open on May 1, 1992, with Cash headlining the first show. But the money ran out. Work stopped in the spring, and by November David Green was bankrupt.

Cash still started performing in Branson in a smaller way, signing on for fifty shows at the Wayne Newton Theater, which seated three thousand. On a good night, Cash might fill half the seats. Some nights, only a few hundred people would show up. According to the theater manager, Cash seemed ambivalent and disinterested during most of his shows there.[2]

Cash on *Zooropa*

When Cash Country failed, Cash had to go back on the road again, which turned out to be a good thing, because it landed him in Dublin, Ireland, on February 8, 1993. While he was there, the rock band U2 invited him into a studio to record lead vocals for a song called "The Wanderer," which became the final track on U2's album *Zooropa*.

Cash and Bono

Johnny Cash had first met Bono, lead singer for U2, in Hendersonville in 1988. As noted a few chapters ago, Bono had watched Johnny Cash's television show when he was just a nine-year-old boy in Ireland, and had been interested in Cash ever since.

Bono recounted later that at the dinner table in his Hendersonville home, Cash said "the most beautiful, poetic grace," thanking God for the food. "Then, when he was done, he looked at me and Adam Clayton and said, 'Sure miss the drugs, though.'"[3]

Afterward, they played some songs together and even started writing one.

Bono had a theological as well as musical interest in Johnny Cash. He called him "a saint who preferred the company of sinners," a man with a deep religious faith who nevertheless embodied all the excesses associated with musical superstardom.[4] That kind of split personality intrigued Bono, and led him to invite Cash to be part of the *Zooropa* sessions.

Zooropa became a number-one album in both Britain and the United States. It sold more than 7 million copies worldwide. Suddenly, a whole generation of music listeners who had never given Johnny Cash a second thought discovered him—and liked what they heard.

Those listeners would soon hear a lot more from him, thanks to something else that happened in February 1993. Just two weeks after his return from Dublin, Cash played a show in Santa Ana, California, and afterward met with a record producer named Rick Rubin.

Johnny Cash performs in Nashville, Tennessee, in 1992.

Rubin, then thirty years old, was the owner of Def American Records, which later became American Recordings. He'd produced acts such as LL Cool J, the Beastie Boys, Run-DMC, Slayer, and the Red Hot Chili Peppers, most of whom Cash was probably only aware of peripherally. It's hard to imagine a less likely producer for anything by Johnny Cash. After all, his most recent concerts had been for dwindling crowds of white-haired tourists at Wayne Newton's Branson theater.

To Cash, Rubin looked like "the ultimate hippie" with his untrimmed beard, long hair, and "clothes that would have done a wino proud."

"I was through auditioning for producers, and I wasn't at all interested into being remodeled into some kind of rock act," Cash wrote. He said he didn't really take Rubin seriously—although he did tell June that he thought Rubin talked "a little like Sam Phillips."[5]

Fortunately, Cash didn't let those initial impressions keep him from continuing to talk to Rubin. Over the next few months, they discussed possible songs for a potential album, and occasionally met in Rubin's Los Angeles home, set up as an informal recording studio, for Cash to play them over.

Cash's contract with Mercury was running out. Pleased with the way his meetings with Rubin had gone, and impressed by Rubin's stated intent to let him be "totally honest," Cash agreed to sign a contract with American Recordings.[6]

"Johnny was made fun of in Nashville for working with me," Rubin said. "It seemed ridiculous to that audience. But he saw the seriousness of what we talked about and could do together—enough to go against those feelings."[7]

American Recordings

American Recordings came out in 1994. It contained more of Cash's own compositions than almost any of his albums of the previous twenty years. The instrumentation was as sparse as it could be: just Cash and his acoustic guitar.

In its marketing, American Recordings played up the dark side of Cash's personal history. The first song released to promote the album was an old ballad about murder called "Delia's Gone." With lyrics updated to include submachine guns, it linked American folk music with modern gangsta rap. In the accompanying, controversial video, Cash tied up model Kate Moss, threw her into a pit, and shoveled dirt over her face. Before the album's release, Cash appeared at in vogue clubs and at South by Southwest, a trendy music festival held in Austin, Texas.

Critics, including those at the highly influential *Rolling Stone* magazine, raved about the new album in a way they hadn't raved about a Cash album in twenty-five years. "I don't think I lost any of my old fans, and I might have gained a few new ones," Cash wrote.[8]

His road shows took on an energy they'd been lacking in recent years. He put the change down to the fact that he was now playing in "young people's places."

"I discovered all over again how it felt to play for a crowd of people with no chairs or tables, standing on their feet, jammed together, energizing each other."[9]

American Recordings made it to number 23 on the country music charts—Cash's highest position in sixteen years. It also won him his first Grammy Award, for Best Contemporary Folk Album, since 1969. His previous win had been for "A Boy Named Sue."

> **Despite the success of *American Recordings*, Cash's career continued to decline in other ways.**

Despite the success of *American Recordings*, Cash's career continued to decline in other ways. The Johnny Cash Museum closed in 1995 after sixteen years. The House of Cash, the gift shop near Cash's home, had once employed more than forty people. By this point, it employed fewer than ten. There was talk of selling it, and within a few years, it, too, would close.

For his second album with American Recordings, *Unchained*, Cash and Rubin took a different approach. They added a backing band, Tom Petty and the Heartbreakers, whom Rubin had first produced in 1994 for the album *Wildflowers*. Rubin also convinced Cash to include songs from many contemporary songwriters, including "Rowboat" by Beck and "Rusty Cage," first recorded by Soundgarden. The other tracks included several of Cash's own compositions, plus some older songs written in the 1950s and 1960s.

Health

Recording was slowed by Cash's ongoing medical problems. Not only did his broken jaw require numerous operations, but he also had begun stumbling and shaking to the point where he was sometimes unable to sing.

But *Unchained* came out in November 1996 to more rave reviews, placing number 5 on *Rolling Stone*'s list of the Ten Best Albums of 1996. In December, Cash received a Kennedy Center Lifetime Achievement Award. He'd been nominated for it by Vice President Al Gore. In February 1998, *Unchained* won the Grammy for Best Country Album. The following year, Cash received a Lifetime Achievement Award at the Grammys ceremony.

Cash's second autobiography, cowritten with Patrick Carr, came out in 1997, capitalizing on the renewed interest in the singer's life and personal struggles.

More Struggles With Health and Drugs

Those personal struggles continued unabated, despite his newfound career success. His daughter, Rosanne, remembers having lunch in New York with Cash, June, and Rosanne's husband, John, and her two daughters after *Unchained* came out. Cash started hallucinating, she said, imagining black puppies in the room. He spilled orange juice in his lap. Rosanne thinks by that time he was once again abusing pain medication.

"It was kind of like that until his death," she said. "He would be lucid, and then he would kind of drift off."[10]

In October 1997, Cash wrote in the paperback version of his autobiography that he suddenly found himself walking backwards on a street in New York, completely involuntarily. He and June contacted a doctor, who examined Cash and told him he needed to go home and go into the hospital right away.[11]

On October 25, in Flint, Michigan, Cash stumbled and almost collapsed as he bent over to pick up a guitar pick. He announced to the audience that he had Parkinson's disease, a slow-progressing disease of the nervous system that impairs movement and over time can make it difficult for a sufferer to walk, talk, or perform other simple tasks. Some laughed, thinking he was joking. He wasn't.

Some laughed, thinking he was joking. He wasn't.

That was the last full-length concert Johnny Cash ever gave.[12]

Following the New York doctor's advice, Cash entered Nashville's Baptist Hospital on October 29. The doctors diagnosed him with a combination of pneumonia, diabetes, and nerve damage. He lapsed into a coma for twelve days, worrying his family so much that June arranged for a special prayer request to be posted to the Johnny Cash Web site.[13]

The next morning, Cash woke up and asked for coffee.

The doctors informed him that he didn't have Parkinson's after all. He had something rarer and worse: Shy-Drager syndrome, which affects the brain and nervous system and usually ends in death a few years after symptoms develop, due to difficulties breathing and swallowing or an irregular heartbeat. Johnny Cash's life expectancy, the doctors told him, was no more than eighteen months.[14]

"I don't have any fear of death," he wrote in an afterword to the paperback edition of his autobiography, written after the diagnosis. "I'm very much at peace with myself and my God . . . I have no regrets, I carry no guilt, and I bear no ill will toward anybody."[15]

Chapter 8

Fade to Black

Cash was released from hospital in early December, and he and June headed off to Jamaica before Christmas. For the next five years, they would spend their winters there.

Cash made a surprise appearance at a Kris Kristofferson tribute in Nashville in June 1998, helping Kristofferson sing "Sunday Morning Coming Down." But mostly he stayed out of public view. That fall he ended up in the hospital with pneumonia again, getting out after ten days but then relapsing and returning to the hospital for most of October.

During that year, Cash began talking to movie producer James Keach about a movie version of his life, to be called *Walk the Line*. Cash and June had become friends with Keach, the husband of actress Jane Seymour, when they had guest starred on Seymour's show *Doctor Quinn, Medicine Woman* a few years earlier. Cash, Keach said, came to him because Cash thought he would make the movie about more than just "sex and drugs and rock-'n'-roll," and would recognize that "his journey as a man and his love with June and the fact that God was at the core of his story."[1]

"We had a very deep spiritual connection," Keach said.[2]

Cash worked closely with scriptwriter Gil Dennis on a script, which was originally sold to Sony and eventually ended up with Fox 2000. Production, however, didn't begin until after Cash's death.

A Final TV Performance

In April 1999, Cash took part in a television tribute to him that included performances by Bruce Springsteen, U2, Emmylou Harris, and Wyclef Jean. Jean's hip-hop performance helped emphasize the link young listeners had found between Cash's image as a rebel and the spirit of rebelliousness inherent in hip-hop.

Cash himself took to the stage to sing "Folsom Prison Blues" and "I Walk the Line." For the first time in nineteen years, Marshall Grant played bass. "He looked road-ready," says biographer Michael Streissguth, but in fact that would be the last performance Cash would give to any audience of a significant size.[3]

He didn't stop working, though. In fact, he worked constantly. He provided songs for the soundtracks of the movies *We Were Soldiers* and *Dead Men Walking*, and more songs to tribute albums for the Louvin Brothers and Hank Williams. And with Rick Rubin's help, he managed to complete a third album for American

Johnny Cash and June Carter Cash at their home in 1999.

Recordings. Released in 2000, it was called *Solitary Man*. Cash wrote three of the songs, cowrote another, and coadapted a fourth. Other songs included Neil Diamond's "Solitary Man" and Tom Petty's "I Won't Back Down." Critical response was positive, but Cash's voice was noticeably weaker this time around.

That weakness frustrated Cash, but Rubin tried to encourage him, telling him that it "didn't sound as though he were tired, it sounded like he was emoting the song."[4]

"If there was a bad day, we would circle back to the material a couple of days later and get a great take," Rubin said of working with Cash as his health deteriorated.[5]

Even though he was declining, his daughter Rosanne feels that his health would have failed much more quickly if not for the recording, and she's grateful. "I think Dad would have gone down like a forty-five degree angle without Rick," she said.[6]

Recording was interrupted twice in October 1999 by trips to the hospital, once for stitches for a gash in his leg, the second for pneumonia.

During the second stay, doctors gave him some good news. He didn't have Shy-Drager's syndrome. Rather, he had something called autonomic neuropathy. That meant his symptoms weren't caused by a fatal disease, but by damage to the part of the nervous system that controls the function the body takes care of without us having to think about them: breathing, sweating, balance, etc.

Press On

While Cash was enjoying a renaissance with his American Recording recordings, his wife, June Carter, took advantage of his spending less time on the road to record her own solo album, *Press On*. It was only the second solo album of her career. The first, recorded in the 1970s and called *Appalachian Pride*, hadn't received much attention.

Cash sang on the album, but it was very much June's record. It mixed familiar Carter Family songs with some she cowrote, and won a Grammy for Best Traditional Folk Album in 1999.

When a reporter asked June if she'd be touring to promote the album, she said, "If we go back on the road, we'll go together. I'll go where he goes, and he'll go where I go."[7]

There would be no more touring for either of them, but June would go on to record a third solo album, *Wildwood Flower*, another mix of Carter Family songs and June's originals, with June and Cash singing together on two songs. It won two more Grammys, for Best Female Country Vocal Performance and Best Traditional Folk Album.

Even as *Solitary Man* was coming out, Cash was collecting and writing songs for yet another album. One was "The Man Comes Around," which he said he spent more time on than any other song he ever wrote. It ended up being the title song of the album. Full of apocalyptic images from the Bible, it talked about what would happen in the times surrounding the prophesied Second Coming of Jesus Christ.

Recording for the new album posed new challenges. Along with all his other physical problems, Cash's eyesight had begun to fail, which meant the lyrics had to be printed out in large boldface type in order for him to be able to read them.

"Hurt"

One of the songs whose lyrics he read was called "Hurt." Written by Trent Reznor for Nine Inch Nails, it's about someone addicted to heroin who hurts himself and everyone around him. Its somber lyrics perfectly suited Cash at that late stage of his life.

> **Its somber lyrics perfectly suited Cash at that late stage of his life.**

"They resonated with him," Rick Rubin said. "I could imagine Johnny Cash singing those words. When he sings them, you think he could have written them."[8]

In fact, a lot of the songs in *The Man Comes Around* were about people leaving or saying good-bye. Once again Cash drew on new material (like "Hurt"), his own songs (like "The Man Comes Around"), traditional songs (such as "Danny Boy"), and old standards (including "We'll Meet Again," made famous during the Second World War by British singer Vera Lynn). *The Man Comes Around* even included a Beatles song, "In My Life."

Photos for the album cover emphasized Cash's age and frailty. And then there was the poignant video for "Hurt."

In the video, images of Cash performing the song with June Carter standing nearby were intercut with film of when he was younger and stronger. Images of the

Cash Museum, not only long since closed but also damaged by a recent flood, emphasized the idea of decay and loss.

When Rosanne Cash saw "Hurt" in Cash's office, she said, "I was devastated. I was crying like a baby." She told her father it was "the most powerful video I had ever seen." In fact, she said, it wasn't a video at all: "It was a documentary."[9]

She also noted that Cash and June seemed unaffected while watching it, viewing it dispassionately with an artist's eye. During filming, Cash reportedly joked around with the crew between the powerful, emotional takes.

On October 17, 2002, the day before the filming, June was diagnosed with a leaking heart valve.[10]

The Man Comes Around came out on November 4, 2002. Later that month, Cash appeared on Larry King's show on CNN, but the interview had actually been taped on October 11. Cash and June headed to Jamaica as had become their custom every winter.

The video for "Hurt" was released in early 2003. *Rolling Stone* called it "one of the most intense and affecting videos in the history of MTV."[11] The album sold more than a million copies: it was Cash's first studio-recorded album to go platinum.

But in January, Cash was once more admitted to the hospital in Nashville with pneumonia. He was back in the hospital in February after cutting his knee, and back again in March after he fell out of bed and passed out.

When he was released, for the first time ever, he was unable to walk out of the hospital. He had to ride out in a wheelchair, and use a walker.

Two days later Cash's sister Louise died. Cash was too ill to attend her funeral.

Losing June

June Carter Cash accepted an award for "Hurt" on behalf of her husband at the 2003 CMT Flameworthy Video Music Awards. She looked unwell. She also seemed to be suffering from some mental confusion, and had trouble delivering her lines.[12]

On April 11, 2003, she was rushed to hospital, where she was diagnosed with congestive heart failure. After a few days, doctors sent her back home to Hendersonville. But twelve days after that, she was back in the hospital.

With her condition worsening, doctors decided the only hope was surgery to replace the defective heart valve. They had to wait a few days, until May 7, because she was taking blood-thinning medication that had to be discontinued long enough for it to clear out of her system.

The operation itself went well. By the next day she was able to breathe on her own. Cash spent several hours with her, talking about what they would do when she was out of the hospital, and his plans to work hard so he could walk unassisted again. But after Cash left, June called Kathy Cash, Cash's second-oldest daughter. She told Kathy she didn't feel she was going to make it and asked her to "please take care of Daddy."[13] Kathy didn't tell her father what June had said, not wanting to worry him.

Early the next morning, June suffered cardiac arrest. Doctors managed to resuscitate her, but it took twenty minutes. She remained in a coma afterward. Cash was called to the hospital. The family gathered. Tests confirmed that there was no brain activity. Although June's body was still alive, her brain was dead, starved by lack of oxygen during the resuscitation attempt. Cash gathered the family in a circle and they prayed. Then he went down to the intensive care unit and gave his permission for the life support system to be switched off.

June Carter Cash died May 15, 2003.[14]

The funeral was held at First Baptist Church in Hendersonville, where Cash and June frequently worshiped. Open to the public, it attracted eighteen hundred people, and was broadcast live on local television. Larry Gatlin, Emmylou Harris, Sheryl Crow, and the Oak Ridge Boys were among those who performed gospel songs.

Rosanne Cash was the only member of the family to speak. She said that June's greatest "mission and passion" was "lifting up my dad."

"My daddy has lost his dearest companion, his musical counterpart, his soulmate and best friend," she said.[15]

Grieving, But Working

As always, Cash turned to work for solace. He recorded more songs and experimented with new sounds. But when he wasn't working, he found life without June very difficult. He had photos of her and letters she had written blown up so he could see them. He had the cover of her *Wildwood Flower* album painted on the elevator in the house. He would pick up the telephone and pretend to talk to her.

Cindy Cash, who had come for what she thought would be a short visit in June, ended up staying until her father died. All of his daughters stayed close to him during the final few weeks of his life. "We had some beautiful conversations in the last few months of his life," Rosanne remembered. "Some of the best conversations of my life."[16]

In June, Cash had traveled to Hiltons, Virginia, the hometown of the Carter Family, where he and June had owned a house. It was the day before June's birthday. Cash performed for a thousand people at the Carter Fold. Two weeks later, he returned and performed seven songs, interrupting a local bluegrass band to do so.

"Despite being crippled, hoarse, short of breath mid-song and profoundly depressed, Cash knew he could still thrill an audience—and he made the unnecessary effort to prove it," wrote Randy Noles, consulting publisher for *Sarasota Magazine*, who was in the audience that day.[17]

A week later in Hendersonville, Cash was visited by Vivian Cash, his first wife. She wanted permission to write a book based on the letters they'd exchanged while he was in the Air Force. Cash agreed.

"It's time," he told Vivian. He even promised to write the foreword. He said he hoped it would be healing for her. They hugged, and Vivian left. "I never stopped loving him," she wrote later. "Through all of it, despite everything, I never stopped loving him for one second."[18]

By August, Cash was nearly blind. But somehow, Cindy Cash said, when she and Cash's sister Reba took him to see June's grave one day, he managed to read the stone and told her, "I'm coming baby. I'm coming."[19]

Early that month, Cash went back into the hospital, but after his release, he started working with a sports physician, Phil Maffetone. Maffetone put him on a healthier diet and started a therapeutic program that soon had Cash walking better than he had in months. Cash thought he might even be able to attend the MTV Music Awards in New York, where the video for "Hurt" was one of the nominees for video of the year. He even booked a flight to Los Angeles for after the awards, planning to resume recording with Rubin.

But MTV told Lou Robin several days before the show that "Hurt" was not going to win video of the year, although it did win an award for cinematography. As it turned out, Cash probably wouldn't have been able to make the event anyway. On Monday, August 25, he was admitted to the hospital again, this time with pancreatitis, an inflammation of the pancreas. He stayed there until September 9.

The End

On September 11, home once again, Cash was working with Maffetone. Suddenly he turned to him and said, "It's time." Maffetone, thinking Cash simply felt like he'd worked enough that day, went back to his hotel.[20]

But that afternoon, Cash was taken ill. His damaged lungs were failing, and he was coughing blood and delirious when the ambulance came. Although he was conscious at the hospital, he couldn't talk. He squeezed the hands of his children, John Carter, Kathy, and Rosanne. As the hours passed, they left his room to try to go get some sleep, with Kathy and Rosanne resting in a glass-walled room nearby, and John Carter on a bed a few floors up.

In the middle of the night, a nurse told Kathy to wake Rosanne, and John Carter was also wakened and brought down from the eighth floor.

> **The three of them comforted their father as best they could.**

The three of them comforted their father as best they could.

At 2:00 A.M., on September 12, 2003, Johnny Cash died.

The private funeral at First Baptist Church featured some of the same musicians who had performed at June's funeral. Emmylou Harris and Sheryl Crow were there. Franklin Graham was there to represent his father, Billy Graham. Kris Kristofferson called Cash "Abraham Lincoln with a wild side."[21]

Fans mourn the loss of country music legend
Johnny Cash. Cash died September 12, 2003.

Cash was buried next to June. Engraved on his grave marker is his name, the dates of his birth and death, and a verse from the Bible, Psalm 19:14: "Let the words of my mouth and the meditation of my heart be acceptable in thy sight, O Lord, my strength, and my redeemer."

Beneath that is Cash's signature.

Chapter 9

The Cash Legacy

In November, as had always been planned, *Unearthed*, a boxed set of five CDs, with an accompanying, lavishly illustrated book that included notes on the songs, was released.

Unearthed featured seventy-seven songs Cash had recorded with Rick Rubin over the previous ten years. Most had never before been released. They included everything from hymns Cash had learned from his mother as a child to songs by Bob Marley, Neil Young, and Steve Earle. For the most part, critics welcomed the set as a fitting capstone to Cash's career, although some accused Rubin of milking Cash's final years for all he was worth.[1]

That same month, a televised tribute aired, hosted by Tim Robbins. It included taped appearances by people as diverse as Whoopi Goldberg, Billy Graham, and Dan Rather.

The Tributes

Tributes to Cash had poured in from the moment he died. New York's *Village Voice* called him "the most important country artist of the modern era."[2] The *Los Angeles Times* said that Johnny Cash not only reshaped country music but was admired by people from "Bono to Dylan to Springsteen."[3]

In Britain, the *Guardian* said Cash was a country musician who was "too big for country music," and that his work would endure indefinitely.[4] And Britain's *Time Out* said, "If America as a nation could speak . . . it would sound something like Johnny Cash."[5] Musicians of all stripes talked about Cash's legacy. Many of their thoughts were published in a special commemorative issue of *Rolling Stone*.

In that issue, Bob Dylan, who had long admired Cash and even recorded with him at one point, called Cash "the greatest of the great then and now."

"Blessed with a profound imagination, he used the gift to express all the various lost causes of the human soul," Dylan said. "Listen to him, and he always brings you to your senses."[6]

> "Listen to him, and he always brings you to your senses."

Kris Kristofferson, who was a janitor in the studio where Cash was recording before his career took off, with a lot of help and support from Cash, said Cash was his hero long before he ever met him. "He represented so much that appealed to me—like freedom. He was willing and able to be the champion of people who didn't have one . . . I think

In November 2003 at the Country Music Awards show, many stars paid tribute to Johnny Cash.

the power of his performance came from the tension between this man who was deeply spiritual and also a real wild man."[7]

"Every man could relate to him, but nobody could be him," Bono said. "To be that extraordinary and that ordinary was his real gift."[8]

"He seemed to be the voice of truth in everything he did," Emmylou Harris said.[9]

Jerry Lee Lewis remembered the early days, when he and Carl Perkins and Johnny Cash were touring together in 1956. "Elvis and them were rockabilly; I was rock & roll," Lewis said. "But we all had country in us, which manifested itself in different ways. If you break it down to the nitty-gritty, we're all country people.

"We were called rebels—I guess because we were."[10]

In an earlier *Rolling Stone* article, Rolling Stones guitarist Keith Richards, who has his own reputation as a rebel, noted that he was "a Johnny Cash freak" when he was young.

"They taught me about the importance of silence in music—that you don't have to play all over the song. You must play what's necessary. If it's done wrong, it can be painfully monotonous. But when it's done right, it has this incredibly powerful focus and intensity, and that's what those early Cash songs were like."[11]

Cash's Ongoing Legacy

Following up on its commemorative issue, *Rolling Stone* published a book, *Cash*, in 2004. The editor, Jason Fine, said Cash's music stood for the simple values of "dignity, compassion for working people and the conviction that music has the power to make our world a better place."[12]

Musically, Greg Kot wrote in the same book, Cash's legacy is the thousands of songs and hundreds of albums he released, "one of the deepest, most far-ranging catalogs in all of popular music."

"No matter what he sang—from the oldest folk hymns and spirituals to rock songs by U2 and Soundgarden—Cash had the unique ability to make it all his own," Kot wrote, adding that Cash had "one of the greatest voices in American music."[13]

The movie version of Cash's early life, *Walk the Line*, came out in 2005. Starring Joaquin Phoenix as Cash and Reese Witherspoon as June Carter, it was both critically acclaimed and a box office success. It was nominated for five Academy Awards and won one. Witherspoon took home the Oscar for Best Performance by an Actress in a Leading Role.

In the movie, Ginnifer Goodwin played Cash's first wife, Vivian. The real-life Vivian died just a few months before the movie came out, on May 24, 2005.

In 2006, Cash's former house on the lake in Hendersonville was sold to Barry Gibb of the Bee Gees for $2.3 million. But Gibb never moved in. The house burned to the ground in April 2007.[14]

In 2006, *American V: A Hundred Highways*, the first posthumous album produced by Rick Rubin, was released. *Rolling Stone* called it "a deathbed benediction." It included Cash's final composition, a "train-song-as-meditation-on-mortality" called "Like the 309." Said *Rolling Stone*: "Cash makes it clear that the prison he always sang about was his mortal body and the world."[15]

A posthumous release of a different kind also came out in 2006. The two-CD set *Personal File* featured forty-nine previously unissued solo Cash tracks. Half came from a session in July 1973, when Cash spent several days recording songs of all kinds and just talking into a microphone about how he felt about the songs.

In 2005, a movie version of Cash's early life was a box office hit. Actor Joaquin Phoenix starred as Johnny Cash.

The tapes were rediscovered in 2004 and compiled by producer Gregg Geller, who has been helping John Carter Cash catalog the hundreds of reels stored in Hendersonville.

John Carter Cash recalled that his father had talked about how he'd made a stripped-down record like his first American Recordings record with Rick Rubin in the 1970s, "but nobody was interested in putting it out."

The archives in Hendersonville contain hundreds of hours of music, not just of Cash's performances but of guests on his TV series, and demos by other artists. There may be many more such recordings to come.[16]

Johnny Cash may be dead, but his voice, "the voice of America," will live on.

Chronology

1932 J. R. Cash is born in Kingsland, Arkansas, on February 26.

1935 Cash and family move to Dyess, Arkansas.

1950 Cash graduates from Dyess High School; enlists in the United States Air Force; in September, he starts training as an intercept radio operator at Keesler Air Force Base, Mississippi.

1951 Cash is transferred to Brooks Air Force Base in Texas; in July, he meets Vivian Liberto.

1954 Receives an honorable discharge at Camp Kilmer, New Jersey; in July, he moves to Memphis, Tennessee; on August 7, he marries Vivian Liberto in San Antonio, Texas.

1955 On March 22, Cash records "Hey, Porter"; in May, he records "Cry, Cry, Cry"; on May 24, first child, Rosanne Cash, is born in Memphis; on June 21, his first single is released.

1956 On April 2, Cash records "I Walk the Line"; on April 16, second child, Kathy Cash, is born in Memphis; on July 7, Cash debuts on *Grand Ole Opry*, where he meets June Carter.

1958 July 29, third child, Cindy Cash, is born in Memphis; on August 1, he starts a new contract with Columbia Records.

1959 On January 1, Cash plays San Quentin Prison in California for the first time; on February 23, he's featured in *Time* magazine.

1960 In June, Cash has his first movie appearance in *Five Minutes to Live*; on August 5, drummer W. S. "Fluke" Holland joins the band, turning the Tennessee Two into the Tennessee Three.

1961 In July, Saul Holiff takes over from Stew Carnall as manager; on August 24, fourth child, Tara Cash, is born in Encino, California; on November 14, Cash is arrested for drunkenness in Nashville, Tennnessee; on December 7, June Carter appears on *The Johnny Cash Show* for the first time, in Dallas, Texas.

1962 On February 11, June Carter joins *The Johnny Cash Show*; in August, he has his first British tour; in November, he plays for troops in Korea.

1964 On March 5, Cash records "Ballad of Ira Hayes"; on July 26, he plays the Newport Folk Festival.

1965 On October 4, Cash is arrested in El Paso, Texas, on drug charges.

1966 On June 30, Vivian Liberto Cash begins divorce proceedings.

1967 On January 11, Cash records "Jackson" with June Carter; on November 2, he's jailed overnight in Lafayette, Georgia.

1968 On January 3, Cash and Vivian's divorce is finalized; on January 13, he records the concert at Folsom Prison, California; on March 1, he marries June in Franklin, Kentucky.

1970 On March 3, Cash's fifth child, John Carter Cash, is born; on April 17, he plays the White House as a guest of President Richard Nixon; on May 24, he appears as a guest of the Billy

Graham Crusade in Knoxville, Tennessee; on October 24, *A Gunfight*, starring Cash and Kirk Douglas, is released.

1971 On February 16, Cash records "Man in Black."

1975 In August, Cash publishes his first autobiography, *Man in Black*.

1977 In May, Cash is awarded an associate degree of theology by Christian International School of Theology; on August 16, he is ordained as a Christian minister.

1978 From February 1 to 5, Cash with Billy Graham in Las Vegas, Nevada; on April 10 and 11, he performs in Prague with daughter Rosanne Cash.

1979 On March 31, the Johnny Cash Museum opens; From June 24 to 27, Cash appears with Billy Graham in Nashville, Tennessee; in December, he records in London with Nick Lowe and Elvis Costello.

1980 On October 13, Cash is inducted into the Country Music Hall of Fame.

1981 In September, Cash is kicked and seriously wounded by an ostrich; on December 21, Cash and his family are robbed by a masked gang in their Jamaican home.

1985 On April 22, Cash has surgery on abdominal scar tissue; in September, he records in Memphis with Carl Perkins, Jerry Lee Lewis, Roy Orbison, and others; in October, *Rainbow*, Cash's last album for Columbia, is released; on December 23, his father, Ray Cash, dies at age eighty-eight.

1988 On December 12, a routine checkup detects that Cash has blocked arteries; on December 19, he is hospitalized for bypass surgery.

1990 March 3–17 and September 17–October 9, the first tours of the Highwaymen take place.

1991 On February 20, Cash wins the Living Legend Award at the Grammys; on March 11, his mother, Carrie Cash, dies at age eighty-six; on May 1, the creation of Cash Country in Branson, Missouri, is announced.

1992 On January 15, Cash is inducted into the Rock and Roll Hall of Fame; in May, the failure of Cash Country is announced.

1993 On February 8, Cash records "The Wanderer" in Dublin for the U2 album *Zooropa*.

1994 April 18–21, Cash films the video for "Delia's Gone" with Kate Moss; on April 26, *American Recordings* is released; October 31–November 8, Cash records the third Highwaymen album in Santa Monica.

1995 In February, *American Recordings* wins the Grammy for Best Contemporary Folk Album; on May 4, Cash cancels his European tour due to complications from jaw surgery.

1996 In November, *Unchained*, Cash's second album with Rick Rubin, is released.

1997 On September 16, Cash tells his band he plans to retire; on October 15, *Cash: The Autobiography* is published; on October 25, Cash performs his final concert in Flint, Michigan.

1998 In February, *Unchained* wins the Grammy for Best Country Album; on June 24, Cash joins Kris Kristofferson onstage in Nashville; August 6, Cash is hospitalized for four days.

1999 In January, Cash receives the Lifetime Achievement Award at the Grammys; on April 6, the All-Star Tribute to Johnny Cash takes place in New York; on October 20, Cash is hospitalized with pneumonia.

2000 In January, Cash starts recording his third album with Rick Rubin; on April 23, Cash receives a Living Legend Medal from the Library of Congress; on May 23, the triple CD compilation *Love, God, Murder* is released by Legacy; on October 17, *Solitary Man* is released.

2001 In February, Cash is hospitalized with pneumonia; on February 21, Cash wins his tenth Grammy, for Best Male Country Vocal Performance.

2002 On October 11, Cash films *Larry King Live*; on October 17, June's leaking heart valve is detected; October 18–19, the video for "Hurt" is shot in Hendersonville; on November 4, *The Man Comes Around* is released.

2003 On September 12, Cash dies of respiratory problems.

Discography

1957   *Johnny Cash With His Hot and Blue Guitar*

1959   *The Fabulous Johnny Cash*

1960   *Songs of Our Soil; Hymns by Johnny Cash; Now There Was a Song; Ride This Train*

1962   *Hymns From the Heart*

1963   *The Sound of Johnny Cash; Blood, Sweat and Tears; The Christmas Spirit*

1964   *Keep on the Sunny Side*

1965   *Bitter Tears; Orange Blossom Special; Ballads of the True West*

1966   *Everybody Loves a Nut; Happiness Is You*

1967   *From Sea to Shining Sea; Carryin' on with Johnny Cash and June Carter*

1968   *Johnny Cash at Folsom Prison*

1969   *The Holy Land; Johnny Cash at San Quentin*

1970   *Hello, I'm Johnny Cash; The Johnny Cash Show*

1971   *Little Fauss and Big Halsy* (soundtrack); *I Walk the Line* (soundtrack); *Man in Black*

1972   *A Thing Called Love; America; Johnny Cash Family Christmas*

1973   *Any Old Wind That Blows; The Gospel Road; Johnny Cash and His Woman*

1974   *Children's Album; Ragged Old Flag; The Junkie and the Juicehead Minus Me*

1975   *Precious Memories; John R. Cash; Look at Them Beans*

1976 *Strawberry Cake; One Piece at a Time*

1977 *The Last Gunfighter Ballad; The Rambler*

1978 *I Would Like to See You Again*

1979 *Gone Girl; Silver*

1980 *A Believer Sings the Truth; Classic Christmas; Rockabilly Blues*

1981 *The Baron*

1982 *The Survivors* (with Jerry Lee Lewis and Carl Perkins); *The Adventures of Johnny Cash*

1983 *Johnny 99*

1985 *Highwaymen* (with Kris Kristofferson, Waylon Jennings, and Willie Nelson)

1986 *Believe in Him; Heroes* (with Waylon Jennings)

1987 *Johnny Cash Is Coming to Town*

1988 *Water From the Wells of Home*

1990 *Boom Chicka Boom; Highwaymen 2* (with Kris Kristofferson, Waylon Jennings, and Willie Nelson)

1991 *The Mystery of Life; Country Christmas*

1994 *American Recordings*

1995 *The Road Goes on Forever* (Highwaymen)

1996 *Unchained*

1998 *VH1 Storytellers* (with Willie Nelson)

2000 *Solitary Man*

2002 *The Man Comes Around*

2003 *Unearthed*

2006 *American V; Personal File*

Glossary

acoustic guitar—A guitar whose sound is amplified only by its own body, not by any electronic means.

album—A collection of recorded songs.

amphetamine—A type of drug that stimulates the nervous system.

concept album—An album whose songs are all built around a particular musical or lyrical theme.

cotton gin—Machinery for removing the seeds from the fibrous balls of cotton plucked from the the plant.

country chart—A list, compiled weekly, of the top-selling recordings of country songs.

electric guitar—A guitar whose sound is amplified electronically.

folk music—Music either directly drawn from or based on music that has been passed down generation to generation by memorization rather than by writing.

gig—Show business slang for a performance.

Gospel music—Music with an explicitly Christian theme, often based on traditional folk music.

Grand Ole Opry—A weekly country music radio program and concert broadcast live from Nashville that is the oldest continuous radio program in the United States, having begun in 1925.

live album—An album recorded at a live concert, as opposed to being recorded in a studio.

manager—The person who oversees a musician's career, booking concerts, arranging tours, and negotiating contracts.

painkillers—Drugs designed to ease pain.

pop chart—A list, compiled weekly, of the top-selling recordings of pop songs.

riding the rails—Jumping aboard a boxcar to get a free train ride to another city where work might be found.

riff—A repeated chord progression, pattern, refrain, or melody.

rockabilly—One of the earliest forms of rock and roll. The name is a mixture of rock and hillbilly, or country, music.

royalty—The percentage of the money earned from the sale of each record that is paid to the artist.

single—A song released to radio on its own, not necessarily as part of an album, although often used to promote an album.

studio—A special room fitted with microphones, recording equipment, and everything else needed to make a record.

Chapter Notes

Introduction

1. Michael Streissguth, *Johnny Cash: The Biography* (Cambridge, Mass.: Da Capo Press, 2006), p. 150.

2. Steve Turner, *The Man Called Cash* (Nashville, Tenn.: W Publishing Group, 2004), p. 124.

3. Greg Kot, "A Critical Discography," in *Cash,* by *Rolling Stone* (New York: Crown Publishers, 2004), p. 188.

Chapter 1. Early Days

1. Steve Turner, *The Man Called Cash* (Nashville, Tenn.: W Publishing Group, 2004), p. 17.

2. Terry Gross, "Interview With Johnny Cash," *Fresh Air* (National Public Radio), August 21, 1998. Retrieved from HighBeam Research, <http://www.highbeam.com/doc/1P1-29111160.html> (October 29, 2009).

3. "The American Experience: Surviving the Dust Bowl: The Great Depression," *PBS.org,* n.d., <http://www.pbs.org/wgbh/amex/dustbowl/peopleevents/pandeAMEX05.html> (May 16, 2008).

4. Ibid.

5. Johnny Cash, with Patrick Carr, *Johnny Cash: The Autobiography* (New York: HarperCollins, 1997), p. 5.

6. Turner, p. 17.

7. Cash and Carr, p. 13.

8. Richard Harrington, "Walking the Line; Johnny Cash's Craggy Legend," *Washington Post,* December 8, 1996. Retrieved from HighBeam Research, <http://www.highbeam.com/doc/1P2-805004.html> (October 29, 2009).

9. Johnny Cash, *Man in Black* (Grand Rapids, Mich.: Zondervan, 1975), p. 24.

10. Michael Streissguth, *Johnny Cash: The Biography* (Cambridge. Mass.: Da Capo Press, 2006), p. 13.

11. Ibid., p. 16.

12. Cash and Carr, pp. 237–238.

13. Turner, p. 20.

14. Cash and Carr, pp. 52–53.

15. Cash, p. 34.

16. Ibid., p. 38.

17. Cash and Carr, p. 37.

18. Turner., p. 23.

19. Ibid.

Chapter 2. The Music Starts

1. Steve Turner, *The Man Called Cash* (Nashville, Tenn.: W Publishing Group, 2004), p. 25.

2. Johnny Cash with Patrick Carr, *Johnny Cash: The Autobiography* (New York: HarperCollins, 1997), p. 50.

3. Terry Gross, "Interview With Johnny Cash," *Fresh Air* (National Public Radio), August 21, 1998. Retrieved from HighBeam Research, <http://www.highbeam.com/doc/1P1-29111160.html> (October 29, 2009).

4. Cash and Carr, p. 53.

5. Gross.

6. Mikal Gilmore, "Man in Black," in *Cash,* by *Rolling Stone* (New York: Crown Publishers, 2004), p 27.

7. Turner, p. 27.

8. Ibid.

9. Ibid., p. 28.

10. Ibid., p. 26.

11. *Johnny Cash: The Man, His World, His Music,* documentary, directed by Robert Elfstrom (Sanctuary, 2005).

12. Michael Streissguth, *Johnny Cash: The Biography* (Cambridge, Mass.: Da Capo Press, 2006), pp. 26–27.

13. Christopher S. Wren, *Winners Got Scars Too: The Life of Johnny Cash* (New York: Dial Press, 1971), quoted in Streissguth, Michael (ed.), *Ring of Fire: The Johnny Cash reader* (Cambridge: Da Capo Press, 2002), p. 23.

14. Gilmore, p. 27.

15. Johnny Cash, *Man in Black* (Grand Rapids, Mich.: Zondervan, 1975), pp. 67–68.

16. Turner, p. 38.

17. Ed Salamon, "Johnny Cash Tells the Stories Behind His Greatest Hits," *Country Music,* July/August 1980, quoted in Streissguth, Michael, *Johnny Cash: the biography* (Cambridge : Da Capo Press, 2006), p. 77.

18. Turner, p. 47.

19. Cash, p. 70.

20. Ibid., p. 72.

21. "The Sun Story," *Sun Records,* February 28, 2008, <http://www.sunrecords.com/content/view/61/75/1/0/> (May 17, 2008).

22. Gross.

23. Ibid.

24. Turner, p. 53.

25. Ibid., pp. 52–54.

Chapter 3. The Hits Begin

1. Steve Turner, *The Man Called Cash* (Nashville, Tenn.: W Publishing Group, 2004), p. 54.

2. Ibid., p. 56.

3. Johnny Cash, *Man in Black* (Grand Rapids, Mich.: Zondervan, 1975), p. 79.

4. Ibid., p. 80.

5. Terry Gross, "Interview With Johnny Cash," *Fresh Air* (National Public Radio), August 21, 1998. Retrieved from HighBeam Research, <http://www.highbeam.com/doc/1P1-29111160.html> (October 29, 2009).

6. Mikal Gilmore, "Man in Black," in *Cash,* by *Rolling Stone* (New York: Crown Publishers, 2004), p. 32.

7. Cash, p. 88.

8. Michael Streissguth, *Johnny Cash: The Biography* (Cambridge, Mass.: Da Capo Press, 2006), p. 71.

9. Cash, p. 85.

10. Ibid., p. 87.

11. Streissguth, p. 71.

12. Turner, p. 61.

13. Tim Perlich, "Johnny Cash: Hard-living Legend Finds Youthful Alternative to Nashville Grind," *New Magazine,* November 21–27, 1996, quoted in Streissguth, Michael, *Johnny Cash: the biography* (Cambridge : Da Capo Press, 2006), p. 49.

14. Streissguth, p. 49.

15. Richard Harrington, "Walking the Line: Johnny Cash's Craggy Legend," *Washington Post,* December 8, 1996. Retrieved from HighBeam Research, <http://www.highbeam.com/doc/1P2-805004.html> (October 29, 2009).

16. Turner, p. 67.

17. Ibid.

18. Ben A. Green, "Johnny Cash Achieves 'Life's Ambition,' Wins Opry Heart," *Nashville Banner,* July 16, 1956, quoted in Streissguth, Michael (ed.), *Ring of Fire: The Johnny Cash reader* (Cambridge: Da Capo Press, 2002), p. 43.

19. Ibid.

20. Steve Pond, "Johnny Cash: The Rolling Stone Interview," *Rolling Stone,* December 10–24, 1992, quoted in Streissguth, Michael, *Johnny Cash: the biography* (Cambridge : Da Capo Press, 2006), p. 75.

21. John Carter Cash, *Anchored in Love: An Intimate Portrait of June Carter Cash* (Nashville, Tenn.: Thomas Nelson, 2007), p. 45.

22. June Carter Cash, liner notes, Johnny Cash: *Love God Murder,* Sony Music, 2000.

23. Ralph J. Gleason, "It Looks As Though Elvis Has A Rival—From Arkansas," *San Francisco Chronicle,* December 16, 1956, quoted in Streissguth, Michael (ed.), *Ring of Fire: The Johnny Cash reader* (Cambridge: Da Capo Press, 2002), p. 46.

24. Robert Johnson, "Gleason Signs Cash for 10 Guest Spots," *Memphis Press-Scimitar,* January 7, 1957, quoted in Streissguth, Michael (ed.), *Ring of Fire: The Johnny Cash reader* (Cambridge: Da Capo Press, 2002), p. 47.

25. Turner, p. 72.
26. Ibid., p. 73.
27. Cash, p. 91.
28. Ibid., p. 75.
29. Streissguth, p. 90.
30. Johnny Cash, with Patrick Carr, *Johnny Cash: The Autobiography* (New York: HarperCollins, 1997), p. 84.
31. Ibid.
32. Colin Escott and Martin Hawkins, *Good Rockin' Tonight: Sun Records and the Birth of Rock 'n' Roll* (New York: St. Martin's Press, 1991), p. 106.
33. "Write is Wrong," *Time Magazine,* February 23, 1959, quoted in Streissguth, Michael, *Johnny Cash: the biography* (Cambridge : Da Capo Press, 2006), p. 75.
34. Turner, p. 40.
35. Streissguth, pp. 95–97.
36. Bob Dylan, "Remembering Johnny Cash," in *Cash,* by *Rolling Stone* (New York: Crown Publishers, 2004), p. 205.
37. Turner, p. 82.

Chapter 4. Downhill Slide

1. Johnny Cash, *Man in Black* (Grand Rapids, Mich.: Zondervan, 1975), p. 93.
2. Johnny Cash, with Patrick Carr, *Johnny Cash: The Autobiography* (New York: HarperCollins, 1997), p. 145.
3. Ibid.
4. Michael Streissguth, *Johnny Cash: The Biography* (Cambridge, Mass.: Da Capo Press, 2006), p. 98.

5. Steve Turner, *The Man Called Cash* (Nashville, Tenn.: W Publishing Group, 2004), pp. 87–89.

6. Ibid., pp. 94–95.

7. Ibid., p. 96.

8. Mikal Gilmore, "Man in Black," in *Cash,* by *Rolling Stone* (New York: Crown Publishers, 2004), p. 37.

9. John Carter Cash, *Anchored in Love: An Intimate Portrait of June Carter Cash* (Nashville, Tenn.: Thomas Nelson, 2007), p. 50.

10. Turner, p. 97.

11. Ibid., p. 98.

12. Ibid., pp. 98–99.

13. Ibid., pp. 103–104.

14. Robert Shelton, "Folk Music: Pompous and Ersatz?" *New York Times,* November 29, 1964, quoted in Turner, Steve, *The Man Called Cash* (Nashville, Tenn: W Publishing Group, 2004), p. 108.

Chapter 5. Clean and Sober

1. Johnny Cash, *Man in Black* (Grand Rapids, Mich.: Zondervan, 1975), p. 138.

2. Christopher S. Wren, *Winners Got Scars Too: The Life of Johnny Cash* (New York: Dial Press, 1971), p. 161.

3. Ibid., p. 130.

4. Steve Turner, *The Man Called Cash* (Nashville, Tenn.: W Publishing Group, 2004), p. 116.

5. Ibid., pp. 116–117.

6. Ibid., p. 118.

7. Michael Streissguth, *Johnny Cash: The Biography* (Cambridge, Mass.: Da Capo Press, 2006), p. 133.

8. Steve Turner, *The Man Called Cash* (Nashville, Tenn.: W Publishing Group, 2004), p. 119.

9. Streissguth, p. 137.

10. Turner, p. 120.

11. Cash, p. 140.

12. Hugh Waddell, ed., *I Still Miss Someone: Friends and Family Remember Johnny Cash* (Nashville: Cumberland House, 2004), pp. 272–273.

13. Johnny Cash, with Patrick Carr, *Johnny Cash: The Autobiography* (New York: HarperCollins, 1997), p. 174.

14. Streissguth, p. 139.

15. Cash and Carr, p. 173.

16. Greg Kot, "A Critical Discography," in *Cash,* by *Rolling Stone* (New York: Crown Publishers, 2004), p. 188.

17. Mikal Gilmore, "Man in Black," in *Cash,* by *Rolling Stone,* p. 39.

18. Cash and Carr, p. 173.

19. W. R. Morris, "Legend Credits Guitarist Established Sound," *Music City News,* May 1979.

20. Streissguth, p. 158.

21. Turner, p. 135.

22. Streissguth, p. 160.

23. Ibid., p. 160.

24. Turner, p. 135.

25. Marion Simon, "Smart Money says Johnny Cash Is the One to Watch This Year," *National Observer,* June 2, 1969, quoted in Streissguth, Michael, *Johnny Cash: the Biography* (Cambridge: Da Capo Press, 2006), p. 75.

26. Turner, p. 136.

27. Tom Dearmore, "First Angry Man of Country Singers," *New York Times Magazine,* September 21, 1969, quoted in Streissguth, Michael, *Johnny Cash: the Biography* (Cambridge: Da Capo Press, 2006), p. 99.

28. Turner, pp. 138–139.

29. Ibid., p. 142.

30. Cash and Carr, p. 206.

31. Streissguth, pp. 170–172.

32. Turner, p. 141.

33. Cash and Carr, p. 207.

Chapter 6. The Low Point

1. Steve Turner, *The Man Called Cash* (Nashville, Tenn.: W Publishing Group, 2004), p. 145.

2. Ibid., p. 146.

3. Johnny Cash, with Patrick Carr, *Johnny Cash: The Autobiography* (New York: HarperCollins, 1997), p. 228.

4. Michael Streissguth, *Johnny Cash: The Biography* (Cambridge, Mass.: Da Capo Press, 2006), p. 184.

5. Robert Hillburn, "Nothing Can Take the Place of the Human Heart: A Conversation With Johnny Cash," *Rolling Stone,* March 1, 1975, quoted in Streissguth, Michael, Johnny Cash: the biography (Cambridge : Da Capo Press, 2006), p. 184.

6. Turner, p. 150.

7. Ibid., p. 161.

8. Ibid., p. 158.

9. Streissguth, p. 204.

10. Ibid.

11. Turner, p. 167.

12. Ibid., p. 168.

13. Cash and Carr, p. 250.

14. Ibid., p. 176.

15. Turner, p. 172.

16. Ibid., p. 175.

17. Cash and Carr, p. 183.

18. Ibid., p. 239.

19. Ibid., p. 236.

20. Turner, p. 179.

21. Robert K. Oermann, "Reporter's Aim Was in Wrong Direction," *The Tennessean,* July 21, 1986, quoted in Streissguth, Michael, *Johnny Cash: the Biography* (Cambridge : Da Capo Press, 2006), p. 227.

22. Cash and Carr, p. 251.

23. Bill Flanagan, "Johnny Cash. American," *Musician,* May 1988, quoted in Turner, Steve, *The Man Called Cash* (Nashville, Tenn.: W Publishing Group, 2004), p. 181.

Chapter 7. **The Final Comeback**

1. Steve Turner, *The Man Called Cash* (Nashville, Tenn.: W Publishing Group, 2004), p. 187.

2. Michael Streissguth, *Johnny Cash: The Biography* (Cambridge, Mass.: Da Capo Press, 2006), p. 236.

3. Bono, "Remembering Johnny Cash," in *Cash,* by *Rolling Stone* (New York: Crown Publishers, 2004), p. 208.

4. Turner, p. 190.

5. Johnny Cash, with Patrick Carr, *Johnny Cash: The Autobiography* (New York: HarperCollins, 1997), p. 253.

6. Ibid., p. 254.

7. David Fricke, "Rick Rubin: The Rolling Stone Interview," in *Cash,* by *Rolling Stone,* p. 146.

8. Cash and Carr, p. 255.

9. Ibid., p. 256.
10. Streissguth, p. 265.
11. Cash and Carr, revised paperback edition, 1998, p. 400.
12. Turner, p. 204.
13. Ibid.
14. Ibid., p. 205.
15. Cash and Carr, paperback, p. 402.

Chapter 8. Fade to Black

1. Steve Turner, *The Man Called Cash* (Nashville, Tenn.: W Publishing Group, 2004), p. 208.

2. Sharon Waxman, "The Secrets That Lie Beyond the Ring of Fire," *New York Times,* October 16, 2005, <http://www.nytimes.com/2005/10/16/movies/16waxm.html> (October 1, 2008).

3. Michael Streissguth, *Johnny Cash: The Biography* (Cambridge, Mass.: Da Capo Press, 2006), p. 271.

4. Turner, p. 211.

5. David Fricke, "Rick Rubin: The Rolling Stone Interview," in *Cash,* by *Rolling Stone* (New York: Crown Publishers, 2004), p. 151.

6. Streissguth, p. 272.

7. Gina Arnold, "She Walked the Line for You Johnny," *The Scotsman,* May 20, 1999. Retrieved from HighBeam Research, <http://www.highbeam.com/doc/1P2-18698407.html> (October 29, 2009).

8. Fricke, p. 151.

9. Turner, p. 216.

10. Ibid., p. 3.

11. Mark Binellli, "Screen Life: Cash's Greatest Film & TV Moment," in *Cash,* by *Rolling Stone,* p. 203.

12. Turner, pp. 4–5.

13. Ibid., pp. 5–6.

14. Ibid., p. 7.

15. Ibid., p. 11.

16. Streissguth, p. 285.

17. Randy Noles, "Unbroken Circle: A Frail and Grieving Johnny Cash Inspired Consulting Publisher Randy Noles and Other Spellbound Fans at His Final Concert in Appalachia," *Sarasota Magazine,* October 1, 2003. Retrieved from HighBeam Research, <http://www.highbeam.com/doc/1G1-108883332.html> (October 29, 2009).

18. Vivian Cash with Ann Sharpsteen, *I Walked the Line* (New York: Scribner, 2007), p. 8.

19. Streissguth, pp. 283–284.

20. Ibid., p. 289.

21. Turner, p. 222.

Chapter 9. The Cash Legacy

1. Steve Turner, *The Man Called Cash* (Nashville, Tenn.: W Publishing Group, 2004), p. 224.

2. Tom Smucker, "Johnny Cash, 1932–2003: Cowboy and Indian, Sinner and Believer, Patriot and Protester, the Man in Black Walks His Final Line," *Village Voice,* September 16, 2003. <http://www.villagevoice.com/2003-09-16/music/johnny-cash-1932-2003/> (October 29, 2009).

3. Zeke Minaya, "Music Legend Johnny Cash Dies at 71," *Los Angeles Times,* September 12, 2003.

4. Adam Sweeting. "Johnny Cash." *Guardian*, September 13, 2003. <http://www.guardian.co.uk/news/2003/sep/13/guardianobituaries.artsobituaries> (October 29, 2009).

5. Ross Fortune, Obituary, *Time Out,* September 17–24, 2003, quoted in Turner, Steve, *The Man Called Cash* (Nashville, TN: W Publishing Group, 2004), p. 223.

6. "Remembering Johnny Cash," *Rolling Stone,* October 16, 2003, <http://www.rollingstone.com/artists/johnnycash/articles/story/5940093/remembering_johnny> (May 15, 2008).

7. Ibid.

8. Ibid.

9. Ibid.

10. Ibid.

11. Jason Fine, ed., *Cash: by the Editors of Rolling Stone* (New York: Crown Publishers, 2004), p. 161.

12. Ibid., p. 16.

13. Ibid., p. 178.

14. David Usborne, "The Flames Went Higher, and It Burns Burns Burns . . . Johnny's House, Destroyed by a Ring of Fire," *Independent,* April 12, 2007, <http://www.independent.co.uk/news/world/americas/the-flames-went-higher-and-it-burns-burns-burns-johnnys-house-destroyed-by-a-ring-of-fire-444311.html> (May 15, 2008).

15. Douglas Wolk, "Johnny Cash: American V: A Hundred Highways," *Rolling Stone,* June 26, 2006, <http://www.rollingstone.com/artists/johnnycash/albums/album/10621325/review/10681037/american_v_a_hundred_highways> (May 15, 2008).

16. David Fricke, "Johnny Cash's Vault Opens," *Rolling Stone,* March 2, 2006, <http://www.rollingstone.com/artists/johnnycash/articles/story/9418830/johnny_cashs_vault_opens> (May 15, 2008).

Further Reading

Books

Cash, John Carter. *Anchored in Love: An Intimate Portrait of June Carter Cash*. Nashville, Tenn.: Thomas Nelson, 2007.

Cash, Johnny. *Man in Black*. Grand Rapids, Mich.: Zondervan, 1975.

Cash, Johnny, with Patrick Carr. *Johnny Cash: The Autobiography*. New York: HarperCollins, 1997.

Cash, Vivian, with Ann Sharpsteen. *I Walked the Line*. New York: Scribner, 2007.

Fine, Jason, ed., *Cash: by the Editors of Rolling Stone*. New York: Crown Publishers, 2004.

Grant, Marshal, with Chris Zar. *I Was There When It Happened: My Life With Johnny Cash*. Nashville, Tenn.: Cumberland House, © 2006.

Neimark, Anne E. *Johnny Cash: A Twentieth-Century Life*. New York: Viking, 2007.

Streissguth, Michael. *Johnny Cash: The Biography*. Cambridge, Mass.: Da Capo Press, 2006.

Turner, Steve. *The Man Called Cash*. Nashville, Tenn.: W Publishing Group, 2004.

Internet Addresses

Internet Addresses

Johnny Cash Online
  <http://www.johnnycashonline.com>

JohnnyCash.com
  <http://www.johnnycash.com>

Rolling Stone: Johnny Cash
  <http://www.rollingstone.com/artists/johnnycash>

Index

A

America: A 200-Year Salute in Story and Song, 89

American V: A Hundred Highways, 129

American Recordings (record label), 105, 107, 112–114, 115, 131

American Recordings (album), 106–108

autonomic neuropathy, 114

B

Barnhill, Jesse "Pete," 21

Beatles, the, 8, 53, 116

Bell, John, 31–32

Bitter Tears, 63

Bono (U2), 78, 103, 126, 127

"Boy Named Sue, A," 76, 107

C

Carnall, Stew, 46, 57

Carter Family, **25**, 45, 59, 61, 62, 79, 80, 91, 115, 120

Carter, June, **25,** 45, 46, 58, 59, 60, 61–62, 63, 67, 70, 71, 73, 74, **75,** 79, 80, 85, 87, **88,** 91, 92, 95, 105, 108, 109, 111, 112, **113,** 115, 116, 117, 118–119, 120, 121, 122, 124, 129

Cash Country, 101–102

Cash, Johnny, **6, 11, 23, 39, 56, 66, 69, 75, 83, 88, 94, 98, 104, 113, 127**

albums, see individual album titles

arrests, 57, 65, **66,** 71

awards, 73, **88,** 107, 108, 118

birth, 10

childhood, **11,** 12–24

country music, 17, 21, 36, 43, 44, 45, 46, 52, 53, 61, 63, 64, 73, 85, 87, 90, 96, 101, 107, 108, 126

death, 122–124

drug addiction, 9, 47–48, 53, 54–55, 57, 58, 59, 65, 66, 67, 70, 71, 72, 77, 80, 83, 84, 86, 90–91, 93, 95, 96, 99, 100, 103, 108

early music career, 32–36, 37–52

education, 16, 23–24, 27, 32

folk music, 48, 52, 53, 62–64, 106, 107, 115, 128

gospel music, 29, 30, 34, 49, 50, 52, 74, 79, 84, 86

high school, **23–25**

illness, 99, 100, 108–110, 111, 114, 115–116, 117–118, 121, 122

injuries, 93, 95–96, 100, 114, 117

marriages, 30, 55, 62, 68, 70, 73, 74, **75**

military career, 27, 28–30

movies, 44, **82,** 83, 85–86, 92–93, 111–112, 129, **130**

music charts, 8, 36, 43, 44, 52, 61, 63, 64, 76, 85, 87, 90, 97, 99, 107

music videos, 99, 106, 116–117, 118, 121

poverty, 12–13

record sales, 8, 51, 87, 90, 117

religion, 17, 19, 30, 41, 73, 74, 81, 83, 84–86, 89, 90, 124

soundtracks, 112

television, 8, 46–47, 48, 53, 58, 59, 65, 76, 77–81, 87, 89, 112, 125, **127**

Cash, Carrie Rivers (mother), 10, 14, 15, 16, 17, 18, 20, 21, 22, 44, 62, 71, 101, 125

Cash, Cynthia "Cindy" (daughter), 51, 120, 121

Cash, Jack (brother), 10, 18–20, 21, 23

Cash, Joanne (sister), 16

Cash, John Carter (son), 59, 80, **88,** 95, 122, 131

Cash, Kathy (daughter), 46, 48, 62, 68, 118, 119, 122
Cash, Margaret "Louise" (sister), 10, 18, 118
Cash, Ray (father), 10, 12–13, 14, 15–17, 18, 19, 20, 26, 43, 62, 97
Cash, Reba (sister), 14, 30, 85, 121
Cash, Rosanne (daughter), 35, 48, 58, 87, 92, 108–109, 114, 117, 119, 120, 122
Cash, Roy (brother), 10, 15, 16–17, 18, 30, 32
Cash Tara (daughter), 58
Cash, Tommy (brother), 18, 44
Cash, Vivian Liberto (first wife), 27–28, 30, 32, 46, 48, **49,** 54, 55, 58, 61, 62, 67, 68, 120, 121, 129
"Chicken in Black, The," 99
Class of '55, The, 97
Clement, Jack, 50, 61, 99
Columbia Records, 8, 50, 51, 52, 58, 61, 87, 91, 97, 98, 99

D
Def American Records, 105
"Don't Take Your Guns to Town," 51–52
Dyess Colony, 12, 13–17, 19, 23, 24, 25, 26, 28, 30, 44
Dylan, Bob, 53, 63, 67, 78, 126

F
Fabulous Johnny Cash, the, 52, 61
Fielder, LaVanda Mae, 22
"Folsom Prison Blues" (song), 38, 42, 43, 112
Folsom State Prison performance, **6,** 7–9, 72, 74, 76

G
Golden Girl, 90
Gospel Road (album), 85, 87
Gospel Road (movie), 85
Graham, Billy, 80, 86, 87, 89, 90, 122, 125
Grammy Awards, 73, 107, 108, 115
Grand Ole Opry, 25, 44–46, 58–59, 77, 86

Grant, Marshall, 7–8, 32, 33, 34, 35–36, 41, 51, 54, 55, 58, 59, 67, 70, 71, 72, 77, 90, 91, 92, 112
Great Depression, 9, 12–13, 46, 52
Great Eighties Eight, 93
Gunfight, A, **82,** 83

H
Harris, Emmylou, 112, 119, 122, 127
Henson, A .J., 24
"Hey, Porter," 30, 34, **35,** 38
"Highwayman" (song), 96
Highwaymen (album), 96, 97
Highwaymen (group), 96–97, **98**
Holiff, Saul, 57–58, 67, 70, 77, 85, 89
Holland, W. S. "Fluke," 65
Hollywood Walk of Fame, **88**
Holy Land, The, 74
Hoover, Herbert, 12
Horton, Billie Jean, 57
Horton, Johnny, 57
"Hurt," 116–117, 118, 121
Hymns by Johnny Cash, 52

I
"I Walk the Line," 31, 40, 43, 44, 45, 46, 51, 65, 112

J
Jackie Gleason Show, 47
Jennings, Waylon, 79, 89, 96, 97, **98**
Johnny Cash and the Tennessee Three, 65
Johnny Cash and the Tennessee Two, 35, 37, 38, 40, 42, 43, 46, 47, 48, 51, 65, 74, 91, 93
Johnny Cash at Folsom Prison, **6,** 7–9, 42, 73
Johnny Cash at San Quentin, 8, 76, 77, 79
Johnny Cash Is Coming to Town, 98, 99
Johnny Cash Museum, 102, 107, 117
Johnny Cash Show, The, 53, 58, 59, 77–81
Johnny Cash Sings Ballads of the

True West, 64

Johnny Cash with His Hot and Blue Guitar, 48

Johnson, Nadine, 23

Johnston, Bob, 8

Junkie and the Juicehead Minus Me, The, 87

K

Keach, James, 111–112

Kilgore, Merle, 60, 61

Korean War, 26

Kristofferson, Kris, 79, 85, 96, **98,** 111, 122, 126

L

Landsberg Barbarians, 31

Law, Don, 50

lawsuits, 42, 50, 91

legacy, 125–131

Lewis, Jerry Lee, 34, 40, 49, 97, 127, 128

Louisiana Hayride, 41, 47

M

Man Comes Around, The, (album), 115, 116, 117

"Man in Black," 80

Mercury, 98, 99, 105

Moore, Sue, 23

N

Neal, Bob, 37, 38, 57

Nelson, Willy, 96, **98**

New Deal, 12, 13

New Johnny Cash Show, The, 89

Nichols, Louise, 23

O

One Piece at a Time, 90

Orbison, Roy, 34, 40, 79, 90, 97

P

Parkinson's disease, 109, 110

Perkins, Carl, 34, 40, 43, 74, 90, 97, 127

Perkins, Luther, 32, 34, 41, 51, 74, 92

Personal File, 129

Phillips, Sam, 33, 34, 35, 43, 44, 48–49, 50, 105

Polygram, 97, 98

Presley, Elvis, 33, 37, 38, **39,** 40, 41, 42, 43, 44, 46, 47, 90, 128

Pride of Jessi Hallam, The, 93

R

Rainbow, 97

Rambler, The, 90

Ridin' The Rails, 89

"Ring of Fire" (song), 60–61

Ring of Fire (album), 61

Robin, Lou, 89, 96, 98, 121

rockabilly, 34, 128

Rockabilly Blues, 91

Roosevelt, Franklin Delano, 12, 13

Rubin, Rick, 103, 105, 106, 107, 112, 114, 116, 121, 125, 129, 131

S

Second World War, 18, 24, 28, 63, 116

Shy-Drager syndrome, 110, 114

Silver, 91

Snow, Jimmy, 84, 85, 86

Solitary Man, 114, 115

Songs of Our Soil, 52

Steve Lawrence Show, 65

Streissguth, Michael, 16, 42, 52, 53, 85, 86, 112

Sun Records, 33, 34, 37, 38, 40, 42, 44, 48, 50, 51, 52, 61, 90, 97, 99

T

tours, 38, 46, 47, 53, 55, 58, 65, 67, 81, 92, 95, 96, 101, 127

Town Hall Party, 48, 50

Twelfth Radio Squadron Mobile (RSM), 27, 28–29

U

U2, 78, 102, 103, 112, 128

Unchained, 107, 108

Unearthed, 125

W

Walk the Line (movie), 44, 111–112, 129, **130**

Water from the Wells of Home, 99

Winston, Nat, 71, 72

Wootton, Bob, 74

Z

Zooropa, 102–103